# SPECTRUM

# Language Arts

# Grade 4

School Specialty
Publishing

Columbus, Ohio

Copyright © 2007 School Specialty Publishing. Published by Spectrum, an imprint of
School Specialty Publishing, a member of the School Specialty Family.

Send all inquiries to:
School Specialty Publishing
8720 Orion Place
Columbus, OH 43240-2111

ISBN 0-7696-8304-5

2 3 4 5 6 7 8 9 10 POH 11 10 09 08 07

# Table of Contents Grade 4

# Table of Contents, continued

# Table of Contents, continued

# Chapter 1

## Lesson 1.1 Common and Proper Nouns

**Common nouns** name people, places, things, and ideas.

> People: teacher, lawyer, baby, uncle, artist, girl, teenager, athlete
>
> Places: school, museum, library, kitchen, store, park
>
> Things: walnut, daffodil, opossum, fence, radio, cottage
>
> Ideas: bravery, fear, happiness, attitude, enthusiasm

**Proper nouns** name specific people, places, and things. Proper nouns are capitalized.

> People: Mandy Lopez, Alex, Aunt Kathleen, Mr. Reichman
>
> Places: Argentina, Windgate Elementary School, Philadelphia Zoo
>
> Things: Timber City County Fair

| Tip | Some nouns are made up of more than a single word: life jacket, polar bear, University of Iowa, Museum of Science and Technology. |
|---|---|

## Complete It

Fill in the blanks in the chart below with the missing common or proper nouns. You may use real or fictional proper nouns.

Example: __President__                    George Washington

| Common Nouns | Proper Nouns |
|---|---|
| teacher | _____ |
| _____ | Duke University |
| singer | _____ |
| father | _____ |
| _____ | Bixby Memorial Library |
| _____ | Mississippi |
| team | _____ |

## Lesson 1.1 Common and Proper Nouns

**Identify It**

Read the following paragraphs. Underline the 22 common nouns. Circle the 14 proper nouns. Remember that a noun can sometimes be more than one word.

The National Museum of American History is located in Washington, D.C. It is run by the Smithsonian Institution. The museum is full of many interesting things. On the second floor, you can see clothes and other items that belonged to First Ladies. Dresses that were worn by Dolley Madison and Nancy Reagan are displayed. You can also see famous flags of the United States. One flag hung over Fort McHenry during the War of 1812.

The museum owns many amazing pieces of history. They own a watch that belonged to Helen Keller, a top hat that belonged to Abraham Lincoln, and boxing gloves that were used by Muhammad Ali. You can send a message by telegraph, or check out the ruby slippers worn by Dorothy in the movie *The Wizard of Oz*. Excitement builds as you realize how many things there are to do and see. Plan to visit the museum for more than one day.

**Try It**

1. Write a sentence about three things you might see in an art museum. Underline the common nouns.

   _____

   _____

2. Write a sentence about a person you would like to interview or a place you would like to visit. Circle the proper nouns.

   _____

   _____

## Lesson 1.2  Pronouns

A **pronoun** is a word that stands for a noun. Using pronouns helps you avoid repeating the same nouns in your writing.

Some pronouns, like *I, me, you, he, she, him, her,* and *it,* refer to a single person or thing. Other pronouns, like *we, us, they,* and *them,* refer to plural nouns.

| | |
|---|---|
| *Carter and Jess* belong to the tennis club. | *They* belong to the tennis club. |
| The cashier handed *the change* to Melissa. | The cashier handed *it* to *her.* |
| *Vijay* lives two blocks away. | *He* lives two blocks away. |

**Possessive pronouns** are pronouns that show ownership. *My, your, his, her, its, our,* and *their* are all examples of possessive pronouns.

   *my* jacket     *your* sister     *our* car     *his* dog     *their* ideas

**Complete It**

Complete the second sentence in each pair with the missing pronoun or pronouns.

1. Ms. Rittenhouse assigned a report to the students in our science class.

   _____ wanted us to research people _____ admire.

2. Harry wrote a biography of Charles Henry Turner.

   When Harry grows up, _____ hopes to become a scientist, too.

3. Charles Henry Turner spent many hours observing insects.

   _____ research proved that bugs can hear.

4. Aliya's report was on Margaret Mead, who studied how the people in other cultures live.

   I think _____ report was one of the most interesting.

## Lesson 1.2 Pronouns

### Identify It

Read the following paragraphs. Find and circle the 19 pronouns.

I am writing a report about Dr. Mae Jemison for my science class. She was the first African American woman to travel into space. In 1992, Mae was aboard the space shuttle *Endeavor* on its eight-day journey. I first learned about Mae Jemison from my dad. He is an engineer at NASA. He met Mae at an awards ceremony a long time ago.

I think that Mae Jemison is an amazing person because of her determination. She graduated from high school and began college when she was only 16 years old. After going to medical school, Mae spent some time working in countries like Cuba, Kenya, and Thailand.

It was not easy for Mae to achieve her dreams. She worked hard and never gave up. Today, she is glad to be a role model for girls all over the world. They can look at Mae Jemison's accomplishments and know that nothing can stop them from reaching their goals.

### Try It

Write two sentences about someone you admire. Use at least one pronoun and one possessive pronoun in your sentences. Circle the pronouns.

_____

_____

_____

_____

## Lesson 1.3  Verbs

**Verbs** tell what happens in a sentence. Many verbs are action words. They tell what the subject of the sentence does.

　　　Emilio carefully *opened* the can.

　　　He *dipped* the brush in the paint and *swirled* it around.

**Solve It**

Write the verb or verbs from each sentence on the lines.

1. Madeleine sang "Yesterday" by the Beatles for the talent show.

　__ ◯ __ __ __

2. Eddie practiced his knock-knock jokes and riddles for weeks before the show. ◯ __ __ __ __ __ __ __ __

3. Erica juggled oranges, eggs, golf balls, and beanbags.

　__ __ __ __ ◯ __ __ __

4. Vinh played two songs on the piano. __ __ __ ◯ __ __

5. Ryan recited three poems from memory.

　◯ __ __ __ __ __ __

6. Lily and Joel danced the tango, the waltz, and the rumba.

　__ __ __ ◯ __ __

7. Miyako showed the crowd her best gymnastics moves.

　__ __ __ __ __ ◯

8. Topher acted out a scene from <u>The Wind in the Willows</u>.

　__ __ ◯ __ __

Write the circled letters from your answers on the lines below.

　__ __ __ __ __ __ - __ __ __

Unscramble the letters to find out what the grand prize was.

　__ __ __ __ __ __ __ __ __

Spectrum Language Arts
Grade 4
10

Chapter 1 Lesson 3
Grammar: Parts of Speech

# Lesson 1.3  Verbs

## Complete It

Complete each of the following sentences with a verb. There may be more than one correct answer, but the verb you choose should make sense in the sentence.

1. More than one hundred people _____ to the talent show.

2. The performers _____ while the audience clapped.

3. The judges _____ they would have a difficult decision to make.

4. While Erica was juggling, she accidentally _____ an egg.

5. Madeleine _____ singing lessons when she was only five years old.

6. Last year, Joel _____ his ankle while he was dancing.

7. Miyako's sister _____ the grand prize at the talent show when she was ten.

8. After the show, the parents and the performers drank punch and _____ cookies.

## Try It

Write a short paragraph about what you and your friends would do if your school had a talent show. Circle the verbs in your paragraph.

_____

_____

_____

_____

_____

## Lesson 1.4  Helping Verbs

A **helping verb** works with the main verb in a sentence. It always comes before the main verb. When words like *am, is, are, was, were, has, have, had,* and *will* are used with a main verb in a sentence, they are helping verbs.

     Marty *is going* to the dentist tomorrow morning.
     The creek *will flood* from the heavy rains.
     Samantha *has read* that book many times.
     The squirrel *was hiding* nuts in the backyard.

**Identify It**

In the sentences below, circle the helping verbs. Underline the main verbs.

1. The first bicycles were invented in the early 1800s.

2. An early type of bicycle was called a *boneshaker*.

3. Many people have contributed to the development of the modern bicycle.

4. Some bicycles were built for two people.

5. Today, postal workers, police officers, and delivery people are using bicycles at work.

6. My family is joining the Ashview Cycling Club.

7. We are planning a weekend trip to some nearby rail-trails.

8. We will ride about ten miles each day.

---

**Tip**

Another word can sometimes come between a helping verb and a main verb. Read carefully to be sure you identify both parts of the verb.
The baby *has* often *dropped* her pacifier under the table.
The Crenshaws *will* probably *come* to dinner on Saturday.

---

## Lesson 1.4  Helping Verbs

**Complete It**
Read the paragraphs below. Fill in each space with a helping verb from the box. You may use some helping verbs more than once.

| is | are | have |
|---|---|---|
| will | had | were |

There are many different kinds of bicycles available today. Deciding how you _____ use your bicycle is an important first step. Mountain bikes _____ designed for off-road biking. They _____ used for riding on unpaved roads and paths. People _____ used bicycles for racing since the late 1800s. Cyclists who _____ competing in a race today want a bike that is light and has many gears. In Europe, many people _____ riding utility bikes. These bikes are strong, sturdy, and practical. A person who _____ carrying a heavy load can depend on a utility bike for a smooth, inexpensive ride.

Some bikes _____ carry more than one person at a time. Tandem bikes _____ built for two people. The largest bicycle ever ridden was a multi-bicycle. A string of 40 people rode it at the same time. If the lead cyclist _____ fallen, the rest of the bikers would _____ been in a lot of trouble!

**Try It**
Write two sentences. Each sentence should have a helping verb and a main verb. Circle the helping verb, and underline the main verb.

1. _____

2. _____

## Lesson 1.5  Linking Verbs

**Linking verbs** link, or connect, the subject of a sentence to the rest of the sentence. The verb *to be* can be a linking verb. Some different forms of the verb *to be* are *is, am, are, was,* and *were*. *Become, feel, seem, look, appear, taste, smell,* and *sound* are also linking verbs.

> Jefferson City *is* the capital of Missouri.
>
> Jackie Robinson *was* the first African-American baseball player in the major leagues.
>
> Stephen Hawking *became* famous for his study of black holes.

As you learned in the last lesson, *is, am, are, was,* and *were* are **helping verbs** when they are used with the main verb in a sentence. When these verbs are used alone, they are **linking verbs**.

(helping verb) (main verb)  (linking verb)

Ms. Bernstein *is helping* us.  Ms. Bernstein *is* my teacher.

### Identify It

In each sentence below, underline the verb. If it is a linking verb, write **LV** on the line. If it is a helping verb that is used with a main verb, write **HV**.

1. _____ Roald Dahl's first book was published in 1966.

2. _____ He was the author of popular books like <u>The BFG</u>, <u>Matilda</u>, and <u>James and the Giant Peach</u>.

3. _____ Roald became friends with Franklin and Eleanor Roosevelt.

4. _____ He appeared funny, kind, and intelligent to fans and readers of all ages.

5. _____ Roald Dahl's children were named Olivia, Theo, Tessa, Ophelia, and Lucy.

6. _____ Today, his books are loved by children all around the world.

7. _____ Dahl's characters become real to readers of his books.

## Lesson 1.5 Linking Verbs

**Complete It**

Read the sentences below. Complete each sentence with a linking verb.

1. The book <u>A Cricket in Times Square</u> _____ by George Selden.

2. Selden _____ a famous children's book writer.

3. After reading <u>A Cricket in Times Square</u> many times, it _____ my favorite book.

4. Chester Cricket, Tucker Mouse, and Harry Cat _____ wonderful characters.

5. I _____ like I know them because they _____ so real.

6. I _____ sure that almost any child or adult would enjoy this book.

**Try It**

Write a short paragraph about your favorite book. Use at least three linking verbs in your paragraph. Underline the linking verbs.

_____

_____

_____

_____

_____

_____

_____

# Review Nouns, Pronouns, and Verbs

**Common nouns** name people, places, things, and ideas. **Proper nouns** name specific people, places, and things. Proper nouns are capitalized.

Common Nouns: elementary school, girl, doctor, country

Proper Nouns: King Elementary School, Elizabeth Li, Dr. Delgado, Greece

A **pronoun** is a word that stands for a noun. The pronouns *I, me, you, he, she, him, her,* and *it* refer to a single person or thing. *We, us, they,* and *them* refer to plural nouns.

Anna plays softball.              *She* plays softball.

Give the tickets to *Mom and Dad.*    Give the tickets to *them.*

**Possessive pronouns** show ownership. *My, your, his, her, its, our,* and *their* are possessive pronouns.

*my* report     *his* sports car     *our* neighborhood     *their* apartment

Some **verbs** are action words. They tell what happens in a sentence.

The man *slips* on the ice.          Amit *laughed* at the joke.

The bell *rang* loudly.

**Helping verbs** are words like *am, is, are, was, were, has, have, had,* and *will.* A helping verb is part of a main verb in a sentence.

(helping verb) (main verb)

The ice-cream truck *has stopped* on our street every day this week.

**Linking verbs** connect the subject to the rest of the sentence. Some linking verbs are *is, am, are, was, were, become, feel, seem, look, appear, taste, smell,* and *sound.*

The peppers *are* spicy.          It *feels* cold in here.

This soup *tastes* delicious.

# Review Nouns, Pronouns, and Verbs

**Putting It Together**

Rewrite each sentence below. Use a proper noun in place of each underlined common noun.

1. The <u>boy</u> was traveling to another <u>country</u> with his <u>uncle</u>.

   _____

2. The <u>school</u> is only one block from the <u>library</u>.

   _____

3. My <u>teacher</u> is taking our class to the <u>museum</u>.

   _____

Read the sentences below. Circle the nouns. Underline the pronouns once. Underline the possessive pronouns twice.

1. The photographer flew to Africa and traveled to many countries.

2. Her grandfather gave her a camera when she graduated from college.

3. Stella photographed animals, villages, children, and landscapes.

Each of the sentences below is missing a verb. The words in parentheses will tell you what type of verb to use to complete the sentence.

1. Stella _____ a photographer. (linking verb)

2. She _____ never traveled to Africa before. (helping verb)

3. Stella's grandfather _____ her to see as much of the world as possible. (action verb)

4. He _____ that we can learn a lot by meeting people who live in faraway places. (action verb)

## Lesson 1.6  Adjectives

**Adjectives** are words that describe nouns or pronouns. Adjectives often answer the questions *What kind? How many?* and *Which one?* Good descriptive words help the reader form a picture in his or her mind.

*yellow* boots     *dangerous* journey     *this* plate     *several* students

An adjective may come before the word it describes, or it may follow the verb in a sentence.

The *roaring* fire made the room feel *warm* and *cozy*.

Isabella's *red* bathing suit stood out against the *pale* sand and the *crisp, blue* sky.

*Four spotted* toads sat on *mossy* logs beside the *shallow* pond.

**Identify It**

Read the diary entry below. There are 22 adjectives. Find and circle each adjective.

Saturday, September 2

Dear Diary,

Today was a strange day. I looked out the window this afternoon and knew a big storm was coming. The sky was dark. A thin, yellow line stretched across the horizon. The air felt sticky and thick.

Suddenly, I heard a loud knocking on the ceiling and the windows. Tiny, icy chunks of hail were falling from the stormy sky. When I looked out the window, I saw the hail bounce off the top of a red car, a city bus, and a large umbrella.

A minute later, the lights went out. Mom put new batteries in our flashlights, and she found some old candles in the junk drawer. We made turkey sandwiches and had a candlelit dinner. The lights came back on just in time for bed. The heavy rain had stopped, and I fell asleep to the quiet pitter-patter of raindrops on the roof of our building.

## Lesson 1.6 Adjectives

**Rewrite It**

Rewrite the sentences below. Include at least one adjective to describe every underlined noun. Try to use adjectives that make the sentences as interesting and descriptive as you can.

Example: The <u>bird</u> sat in the <u>tree</u>.

<u>The cheerful red bird sat in the gnarled old tree.</u>

1. The <u>girl</u> put on her <u>raincoat</u> and <u>boots</u>.

   _____

2. After the <u>snowstorm</u>, the <u>plows</u> cleared the <u>streets</u>.

   _____

3. A <u>rainbow</u> appeared in the <u>sky</u> behind the <u>house</u>.

   _____

4. The <u>farmer</u> and his family took shelter from the <u>tornado</u> in the <u>basement</u>.

   _____

   _____

**Try It**

Write about an experience you have had with the weather. You might write about a thunderstorm, a snowstorm, a sunny day, or a drought. Use at least five adjectives in your paragraph. Circle the adjectives.

_____

_____

_____

# Lesson 1.7 Adverbs

**Adverbs** are words that describe verbs, adjectives, and other adverbs. Many adverbs end with the letters **ly**. Adverbs often answer the questions *When? Where? How?* or *How much?*

> Raymond *easily* sank the basketball. (*Easily* describes the verb *sank* by telling how.)
>
> We were *too* late to see the movie. (*Too* describes the adjective *late* by telling how.)
>
> Alicia should arrive *very soon*. (*Soon* describes the verb *arrive* by telling when. *Very* describes the adverb *soon* by telling how.)

To decide whether a word is an adverb, find the word it modifies, or describes. If it answers the questions *What kind? How many?* or *Which one?* the word is probably an adjective. If it tells *When? Where? How?* or *How much?* it is probably an adverb.

## Identify It

Read the paragraphs below. Find and circle the 11 adverbs. Then, draw an arrow from each adverb to the word it modifies, or describes.

Earthworms should be welcomed eagerly into any garden. They eat soil and make tunnels. The worms digest the soil, and the waste material they leave behind is called *castings*. These castings are extremely good for the soil. They make it very rich in nutrients. The tunnels earthworms patiently dig are good for the soil. They allow oxygen and nutrients to travel easily to the plant's roots. Soil that is packed loosely allows water to drain quickly.

Earthworms are amazing in many other ways, too. If a worm is accidentally cut in half by a shovel or a rake, it can grow a completely new back half! Worms are incredibly strong, too. A worm the size of a human being would be about 1,000 times stronger than that human!

## Lesson 1.7 Adverbs

**Solve It**

Underline the adverb or adverbs in each sentence. Then, search for the 11 adverbs in the word search puzzle. Circle each adverb you find in the puzzle.

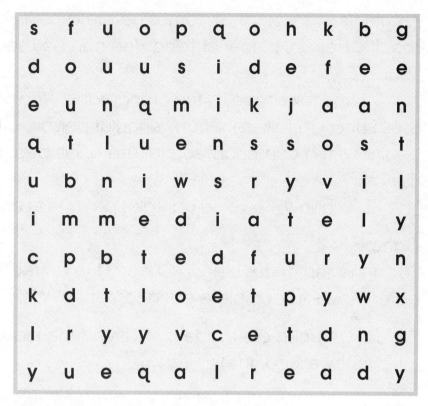

| s | f | u | o | p | q | o | h | k | b | g |
|---|---|---|---|---|---|---|---|---|---|---|
| d | o | u | u | s | i | d | e | f | e | e |
| e | u | n | q | m | i | k | j | a | a | n |
| q | t | l | u | e | n | s | s | o | s | t |
| u | b | n | i | w | s | r | y | v | i | l |
| i | m | m | e | d | i | a | t | e | l | y |
| c | p | b | t | e | d | f | u | r | y | n |
| k | d | t | l | o | e | t | p | y | w | x |
| l | r | y | y | v | c | e | t | d | n | g |
| y | u | e | q | a | l | r | e | a | d | y |

1. Your garden already has some earthworms, but you can easily add more.

2. Go outside at night, and bring a flashlight with you.

3. Walk very quietly so that you do not wake your neighbors.

4. If you find a worm inside its hole, gently dig it out.

5. If you go earthworm hunting immediately after a storm, you will quickly find many worms.

6. After you release the worms in your garden, the soil will become richer.

**Try It**

Imagine that you had a friend who had never seen a worm before. How would you describe it? Write several sentences that describe how worms look, feel, move, and so on. Use at least two adverbs in your description. Circle the adverbs.

_____

_____

## Lesson 1.8 Articles

An **article** is a word that comes before a noun. Use *the* to talk about a specific person, place, or thing. *The* can be used with a singular or plural noun.

> *the* telescope   *the* orangutan   *the* goldfish   *the* skateboards

Use *a* or *an* to talk about any singular person, place, or thing. If the noun begins with a consonant sound, use *a*. If it begins with a vowel sound, use *an*.

> *a* **p**illow        *a* **c**antaloupe        *an* **o**ctopus        *an* **e**arring

### Complete It

Read the sentences below. Choose the correct article from the pair in parentheses to complete each sentence. Write it in the space.

1. Totem poles are made by Native American tribes of _____ Pacific Northwest. (a, the)

2. _____ colors that are most often used in the Northern style are red, black, and turquoise. (The, An)

3. A totem pole might tell _____ family legend. (a, an)

4. Some poles tell the story of _____ important event. (a, an)

5. It can take _____ artist nine months to carve a totem pole. (an, a)

6. Many people think of a totem pole as _____ piece of art. (an, a)

---

**Tip**

When deciding to use *a* or *an*, remember to pay attention to the sound at the beginning of a word, not just the first letter of the word.
*Hour* begins with the consonant **h** but has a vowel sound **ow**.
Use the article *an—an hour*.
*Unit* begins with the vowel **u** but has a consonant sound **y**.
Use the article *a—a unit*.

---

## Lesson 1.8  Articles

**Proof It**

Read the paragraphs below. Find and circle the 28 articles. Twelve of the articles are incorrect. Use proofreaders' marks to correct them.

| | |
|---|---|
| ℮ | – **delete** |
| ^ | – **insert** |

Totem poles can be a reminder of an family's history. The carved human and animal figures tell the story of a family's ancestors. Each animal has the special meaning to an tribe. An order of the animals on the pole is also important. An interpreter, or a expert in an culture, can help explain the meanings of a symbols. For example, a animal like a coyote can be a symbol of a trickster. A eagle represents courage or bravery. A bear is a caring figure.

Sadly, very few of an oldest totem poles still exist today. A weather in the Northwest is rainy and moist. Most totem poles have rotted after spending long years in the rain and wind. The few poles that have been saved can be viewed at museums like a Royal British Columbia Museum.

**Try It**

1. Make a list of five animals or figures you would include if you made a totem pole. Be sure to use the correct article before each item.

_____

_____

2. Write a sentence that includes all three articles.

_____

_____

# Review Adjectives, Adverbs, and Articles

**Adjectives** describe nouns or pronouns and answer the questions *What kind? How many?* or *Which one?*

> The *sparkling* stars lit the *night* sky.
>
> The *enormous* watermelon was *cool* and *refreshing*.

**Adverbs** describe verbs, adjectives, and other adverbs. Adverbs often answer the questions *When? Where? How?* or *How much?*

> Alla *cheerfully* smiled for the camera.
>
> I will write you a letter *soon*.
>
> Jason was *too* tired to watch the end of the movie.

An **article** is a word that comes before a noun. *The* refers to a specific person, place, or thing. *A* or *an* refer to any person, place, or thing. Use *a* with words that begin with a consonant sound. Use *an* with words that begin with a vowel sound.

> *the* subway      *the* astronauts      *a* **f**ootball      *an* **a**ccident

## Putting It Together

Fill in each space below with the correct article.

1. A firefighter is _____ person who is trained to put out fires and rescue people.

2. Firefighters try to take away _____ things a fire needs to burn: fuel, heat, and oxygen.

3. Sometimes water is used to put out _____ fire, and sometimes _____ type of foam is used.

4. In _____ emergency, firefighters must think and act quickly.

5. _____ alarm alerts firefighters that there is _____ fire.

6. It is important to test _____ batteries several times a year in a home fire alarm.

# Review Adjectives, Adverbs, and Articles

Read the sentences below. Circle the 12 adjectives you find. Underline the 7 adverbs.

1. Firefighting can be exciting, but it is a difficult job.

2. The temperature inside burning buildings can be extremely high.

3. Experienced firefighters can work quickly and calmly.

4. They often work long shifts, so they spend many hours together.

5. These brave men and women must be in excellent shape.

6. Many firefighters proudly say that they have the best job in the world.

Rewrite the sentences below. If *adj.* is at the end of the sentence, add an adjective to describe the underlined word. If *adv.* is at the end of the sentence, add an adverb to describe the underlined word.

1. The <u>fire engine</u> raced down the street. (*adj.*)

   _____

2. The firefighter <u>stepped</u> over the hose. (*adv.*)

   _____

3. The firehouse's Dalmatian <u>barked</u> as the alarm sounded. (*adv.*)

   _____

4. The <u>firefighter</u> put on his oxygen mask and nodded to his partner. (*adj.*)

   _____

   _____

## Lesson 1.9 Prepositions

A **preposition** is a word that connects a noun or a pronoun to another part of the sentence. Every preposition has an object. If you are not sure whether a word is a preposition, remember to look for its object.

Some common prepositions are *at, in, on, to, for, into, onto, with, under, over, before, during, after,* and *across.* In the examples below, the prepositions are in bold print. The objects are underlined.

> The tools are **in** <u>the basement</u>.
> The kiwis are **on** <u>the kitchen table</u>.
> Quinn and Ann are **at** <u>the movies</u>.
> Put away your bikes **before** <u>the storm</u>.
> Miguel waited **for** <u>three hours</u>.

### Identify It

In each sentence below, circle the preposition. Then, underline the object.

1. Yesterday was Pajama Day at school.

2. Terrell looked in his dresser drawer.

3. He decided to wear striped pajamas for Pajama Day.

4. He searched everywhere and finally found his slippers under the bed.

5. His sister, Erika, wore a bathrobe over her pajamas.

6. Terrell and Erika climbed onto the bus and laughed when they saw what their friends were wearing.

| Tip | The word *to* is not always a preposition. When *to* comes before a verb, it is part of the verb. prep.                              verb I am going *to* the basketball game. I would like *to meet* your sister. |
| --- | --- |

## Lesson 1.9  Prepositions

**Complete It**

Complete the sentences below with prepositions from the box. Some prepositions may be used more than once.

| for | under | across | with | to |
|-----|-------|--------|------|-----|
| in | on | at | during | |

1. Ms. Molina wore curlers _____ her hair.

2. _____ lunchtime, the cafeteria served pancakes _____ eggs.

3. Terrell ate lunch _____ Michael, Antonio, Eliza, and Seeta.

4. Ms. Molina's students felt silly playing kickball _____ their pajamas _____ recess.

5. Terrell made it _____ third base when he kicked the ball _____ the field.

6. Jana and Maddy put their stuffed animals _____ their desks.

7. Two sixth graders took photos _____ the school newspaper.

8. Terrell's friend Michael dropped his toothbrush _____ his desk.

**Try It**

Write a short paragraph about a special day or event at your school. Use at least four prepositions in your paragraph. Circle the prepositions.

_____

_____

_____

_____

## Lesson 1.10  Conjunctions

A **conjunction** is a connecting word. It can join words, sentences, or parts of sentences. Some common conjunctions are *and, or, but,* and *because.*

Rachael *and* Colin rode the bus to the YMCA.

Will the Bengals *or* the Broncos win the game?

I like going to the pool, *but* I would rather swim at the beach.

Kenji ran back inside the apartment *because* he forgot his lunch.

**Complete It**

Read the advertisement below. Circle the conjunction in parentheses that best completes each sentence.

## VISIT HARBOR SPRINGS AMUSEMENT PARK!

Do you like fast rides, (and, or) would you rather test your game skills?

We have two new roller coasters, a wave pool, (or, and) many activities for little ones.

Families come to Harbor Springs Park (or, because) they know they'll have a great time.

We are not the biggest park in the state, (but, or) we are the best!

Children under five (because, and) senior citizens get in for free.

Visitors who arrive before 11 A.M. receive a free water bottle (and, but) $2 off admission.

Hours: Monday–Thursday 9:30 A.M.–10 P.M.

Friday, Saturday, (and, or) Sunday  9 A.M.–11 P.M.

## Lesson 1.10  Conjunctions

**Identify It**

Read the letter below. Find and circle the 11 conjunctions.

July 14

Dear Haley,

Are you having a good summer? I can't believe it's already July, but I am glad there is still another month of vacation left. Last weekend, Eva, Dad, and I went to Harbor Springs Amusement Park. The park was crowded because it was such a nice day. Eva and Dad loved a roller coaster called "the Quicksilver," but I liked the Ferris wheel best. I rode it four times. I would have kept going, but it was time for lunch.

I think I like Ferris wheels because you can see so far when you reach the top. Did you know that the first Ferris wheel carried 2,160 people and weighed 2,200 tons? I wish I could take a ride on it, but it was built for the World's Fair in 1893. Maybe someday I can go to Japan and ride the Sky Dream Fukuoka. It is one of the biggest Ferris wheels in the world.

Write back to me or call soon. I can't wait to see you in August!

Your best friend,

Lola

**Try It**

If you could invent an amusement park ride, what would it be like? Describe your ride using at least two conjunctions in your answer.

_____

_____

_____

_____

# Review Prepositions and Conjunctions

A **preposition** connects a noun or a pronoun to another part of the sentence. *At, in, on, to, for, into, onto, with, under, over, before, during, after,* and *across* are prepositions. To be sure a word is a preposition, look for its object in the sentence.

> Jonathan played a board game **with** his parents **on** Saturday night.
> The coach gave the players a pep talk **before** the game.
> Ellie ran **across** the yard and jumped **in** the pool.

A **conjunction** joins words, sentences, or parts of sentences. *And, or, but,* and *because* are common conjunctions.

> Ms. Cree loves strawberries, *but* she is allergic to them.
> Will *and* Amber sat on the porch *because* it was hot inside.

## Putting It Together

Read the sentences below. If the underlined word is a preposition, write *prep.* on the line. If it is a conjunction, write *conj.* on the line.

1. _____ The Iditarod is a sled-dog race <u>across</u> Alaska.

2. _____ The mushers <u>and</u> their teams of dogs must be ready for all kinds of conditions.

3. _____ They race <u>from</u> Anchorage to Nome.

4. _____ The first Iditarod was held <u>in</u> 1973.

5. _____ Thirty-five mushers entered the race, <u>but</u> thirteen of them did not finish.

6. _____ Most mushers use Alaskan huskies <u>because</u> they are strong and hardworking.

7. _____ <u>After</u> a race, the mushers and their dogs are eager to relax and get warm.

# Review Prepositions and Conjunctions

Read the paragraphs below. Circle the nine conjunctions. Underline the 19 prepositions.

The Iditarod is not an easy race for anyone. Can you imagine how much harder it would be for a person who could not see? There are many challenges during the race. Mushers must face the cold, the distance, problems with the dogs, and bad weather. In March 2004, Rachael Scdoris and her dogs waited at the starting line in Anchorage, Alaska. Rachael is blind, but she knows she can do anything she wants. She just has to work a little harder sometimes.

Rachael's guide, Paul, was always in touch with her by radio. He gave her directions for leading the team over a hill or under a bank of trees. Rachael raced for 750 miles. Then, she made the hard decision to quit, or *scratch*, 400 miles from the finish line. Five of her dogs were sick and were losing weight. Rachael knew that the health of her dogs was more important than the race.

Rachael is the first blind musher to try to run the Iditarod, but she doesn't want to be remembered because she is blind. Rachael wants to be remembered because she is a good athlete with a big heart.

In each sentence below, circle the preposition. Then, underline the object.

1. Rachael Scdoris was born in Oregon.

2. She carried the torch to the Salt Lake City Winter Olympics.

3. Rachael feels a strong bond with her dogs.

4. The dogs pull the sled quickly across the frozen ground.

## Lesson 1.11 Declarative and Imperative Sentences

A **declarative sentence** is a statement. It begins with a capital letter and ends with a period. A statement gives information.

**K**yra and Whitney are twins.     **C**han's painting is not dry yet.
**M**aine is well known for its lobster.

An **imperative sentence** is a command. Use a command to request something. A command also begins with a capital letter and ends with a period.

**D**on't forget to bring the bag.     **P**ut the bread on the counter.
**L**eave your umbrella in the hallway.
**R**ead the first two pages.

### Identify It

Read each sentence below. Write **D** in the space if it is a declarative sentence. Write **I** if it is an imperative sentence.

1. _____ Pizza is a favorite food all around the world.

2. _____ Make your own pizza at home with just a few ingredients.

3. _____ You can use pita bread or an English muffin for the crust.

4. _____ Have an adult chop vegetables like peppers and olives.

5. _____ Spread some tomato sauce on the bread, and add your toppings.

6. _____ Most people use mozzarella cheese, but some like provolone.

7. _____ Sprinkle the cheese on top of your pizza, and bake it until the topping is bubbly.

**Tip**

**Statements** usually begin with a noun or a pronoun.
*The characters* in my favorite book are named Milo and Flannery.
**Commands** often begin with a verb.
*Look* at the rabbit hiding in the bushes.

# Lesson 1.11 Declarative and Imperative Sentences

## Proof It

Some of the sentences in the paragraphs below are missing periods. Use proofreaders' marks to add the missing periods. Then, find the two imperative sentences and underline them.

⊙ – insert period

Pizzas have a long history in Europe The first written history of Rome, from 300 B.C., had a description of a flat bread with olive oil, herbs, and other toppings. The first pizzeria was in Naples, Italy It opened in 1830 and is still in business today! Visit this shop for a taste of a real Italian pie

In 1905, an Italian immigrant opened the first pizza shop in America. It was called Lombardis The shop was located in New York City. The pizza was popular, but most of the customers were other Italians It took a few decades for the rest of America to learn to love this hot, cheesy food.

By the 1950s, pizza chains started opening around the country Pizza could be made quickly and delivered to people's homes. Everyone loved the convenience. People also liked ordering a pizza just the way they wanted it Order a pizza today, or make one of your own. You will experience a little bit of food history with every bite

## Try It

1. Write a command you might find in a recipe for making pizza.

_____

2. Write a statement about your favorite food.

_____

# Lesson 1.12 Interrogative and Exclamatory Sentences

An **interrogative sentence** is a question. A person asks a question to find more information about something. An interrogative sentence begins with a capital letter and ends with a question mark.

> **D**id you take the subway**?**　　　**W**here will the new library be**?**
> **C**an we go canoeing on Saturday**?**

An **exclamatory sentence** shows excitement, surprise, or strong feelings. An exclamatory sentence begins with a capital letter and ends with an exclamation point.

> **T**he dog got out**!**　　　　　　**T**here is a bug in your hair**!**
> **T**he shuttle has to make an emergency landing**!**

Sometimes, an exclamation can be a single word. Sometimes, it can contain a command.

> Surprise!　　Uh-oh!　　Help!　　Look out!　　Play ball!　　Come here!

## Complete It

The sentences below are missing end marks. Add a question mark to the end of interrogative sentences. Add an exclamation point to the end of exclamatory sentences.

1. Have you ever heard of Roberto Clemente__

2. He was one of the best outfielders of all time__

3. Did Roberto play for any teams other than the Pittsburgh Pirates__

4. How many schools in the United States are named after Roberto Clemente__

5. "Clemente is the best__" shouted a fan after the Pirates beat the Orioles in the 1971 World Series.

6. Did you know that Roberto did a lot of charity work during the off-season__

## Lesson 1.12 Interrogative and Exclamatory Sentences

**Rewrite It**

Rewrite each sentence below. If there is an **I** after the sentence, rewrite it as an interrogative sentence. If there is an **E** after the sentence, rewrite it as an exclamatory sentence.

Example: Roberto Clemente was born on August 18, 1934. (I)

**When was Roberto Clemente born?** _____

1. Roberto Clemente was born in Carolina, Puerto Rico. (I)

_____

2. He was elected to the National Baseball Hall of Fame in 1973. (I)

_____

3. During his career, Roberto had 3,000 hits. (E)

_____

4. Roberto was only 38 years old when he died in a plane crash. (I)

_____

5. He was on his way to help the victims of an earthquake in Nicaragua. (I)

_____

6. He earned 12 Gold Glove awards in a row. (E)

_____

**Try It**

Think of a famous athlete. Now, write two questions you would like to ask that athlete.

_____

_____

NAME _____

## Review Sentence Types

**Declarative sentences** and **imperative sentences** both begin with a capital letter and end with a period. A declarative sentence is a statement that gives information. An imperative sentence is used to give a command or request something.

| Declarative Sentences | Imperative Sentences |
|---|---|
| Male cardinals are bright red. | Answer the phone. |
| Lydia has curly brown hair. | Wear your new jeans. |

An interrogative sentence asks a question. It begins with a capital letter and ends with a question mark.

What is the capital of Georgia? How old will Kent be this year?

An exclamatory sentence shows excitement, surprise, or strong feelings. It begins with a capital letter and ends with an exclamation point.

We need help! Amina got a puppy today!

**Putting It Together**

Read each sentence below, and decide what type of sentence it is. Write **D** if it is a declarative sentence, **IMP** if it is an imperative sentence, **INT** if it is an interrogative sentence, and **E** if it is an exclamatory sentence.

1. _____ The bus dropped off Hiroshi, Jacob, Teresa, and Grace at the community center.

2. _____ The center was putting on a play.

3. _____ Have you ever heard of the play The Princess and the Pea?

4. _____ Hiroshi and Grace hoped to get small roles, and Teresa tried out for the lead.

5. _____ Look at the cast list on the bulletin board.

6. _____ "I got the part!"

## Review Sentence Types

Read the sentences below. If the end mark is correct, make a check mark on the line. If the end mark is not correct, delete it ( ℓ ) and write the correct end mark on the line.

1. Grace was nervous because she had never performed in front of a crowd? __

2. Mrs. Wilmott asked, "Jacob, will you help paint the scenery for the play?" __

3. Jacob exclaimed, "I'd love to." __

4. Teresa wondered, "How many performances will there be?" __

5. The play will open on March 8! __

6. This will be the best play in the history of Longwood Community Center! __

7. Buy tickets early to make sure you get a good seat? __

1. Imagine that it was your job to review the community center's play. Write a declarative sentence that describes your thoughts about it.

   _____

2. Imagine that you are the director of a play. Write an imperative sentence that you might say to one of your actors.

   _____

3. What do you think people will say when the play is over? Write an exclamatory sentence on the line.

   _____

# Lesson 1.13 Parts of a Sentence: Subject

The **subject** of a sentence is what a sentence is about. A subject can be a single word, or it can be several words.

> *You* need to wear a hat and mittens.
>
> *Daffy Duck* first appeared in a cartoon in 1937.
>
> *Toddy, Jenny, Sonia,* and *Lisa* have been friends for years.

In a statement, the subject is found before the verb.

(subject)      (verb)

*The cricket team won* four matches in a row.

To find the subject in a question, ask yourself *Who?* or *What?* the sentence is about. Try turning the question into a statement to double-check your answer.

> Where is *the stadium* located?    *The stadium* is located where.

**Identify It**

Circle the subject in each sentence below.

1. The papaya is also called a pawpaw fruit.

2. It has sweet pink or yellow flesh and many small, black, peppery seeds.

3. The skin of a kiwi is fuzzy and brown.

4. Mangoes grow in tropical climates all around the world.

5. Have you ever heard of ugli fruit?

6. It is a combination of a grapefruit and a tangerine.

| Tip | A command usually begins with a verb. The subject is understood to be *you,* even if the word *you* is not in the sentence. Put the flowers in the vase.   (You) put the flowers in the vase. Leave the map in the car.   (You) leave the map in the car. |
| --- | --- |

# Lesson 1.13 Parts of a Sentence: Subject

## Complete It

Each sentence below is missing a subject. Find the subject in the box that best fits each sentence and write it on the line.

| | | |
|---|---|---|
| **A breadfruit tree** | **Benjamin** | |
| **Monkeys** | **Lucy and Connor** | **The insides of coconuts** |
| **The peanut butter fruit** | **Passion fruit juice** | |

1. _____ worked together to make a fruit salad with five kinds of tropical fruits.

2. _____ are used to harvest coconuts in some places because they climb trees easily.

3. _____ are filled with hard, white flesh and sweet "coconut water."

4. _____ can produce more than 800 pieces of fruit in one season!

5. _____ can be a refreshing drink on a hot summer day.

6. _____ cut open a star fruit and tasted one of the star-shaped slices.

7. _____ grows in Central and South America and tastes like peanut butter.

## Try It

1. Write a sentence in which "understood *you*" is the subject.

_____

2. Write a sentence describing a type of fruit. Underline the subject.

_____

# Lesson 1.14 Parts of a Sentence: Predicate

A **predicate** tells what the subject of a sentence is or does. The predicate always includes the verb. Finding the verb can help you identify the predicate.

In the sentences below, the verbs are in bold. The predicates are in italics.

> Quan's grandparents **live** *in Vietnam.*
> The Johnsons **brought** *a kite to the park.*
> My aunt and uncle **have** *a rooftop garden.*

## Identify It

In each sentence below, underline the complete predicate. Then, circle the verb.

On a sunny Saturday afternoon, Tierra and Cody walked to the library. They passed the recreation center, their school, and Burnside Park. Cody waved to Mr. Crockett. Every weekend, he and his dad bought peanuts for the ducks from Mr. Crockett.

Tierra and Cody crossed the street at the crosswalk. They walked past the large lions and up the library's wide marble stairs. Inside the building, Tierra and Cody paused in the cool, dim entryway. Their favorite tradition was throwing a few pennies into the wishing pond. Neither Tierra nor Cody told anyone their library wishes. They put away their change. Then, they headed toward the children's section and Mrs. Winklebaum's desk.

# Lesson 1.14  Parts of a Sentence: Predicate

## Match It

One box below is filled with subjects. One box is filled with predicates.
Match each subject to a predicate. Then, write the complete sentences
on the lines below.

| Subjects | Predicates |
|---|---|
| Mrs. Winklebaum | are members of the Bookworm Summer Reading Club. |
| The library | likes to read books about dinosaurs and ancient cities. |
| Tierra and Cody | were stacked on the librarian's desk. |
| Cody | was built in 1911. |
| Many books and papers | gave Tierra and Cody a stamp for each book they read. |

1. _____

2. _____

3. _____

4. _____

5. _____

## Try It

Write a short paragraph about a person or place in your community.
Underline the predicate in each sentence.

_____

_____

_____

## Lesson 1.15  Parts of a Sentence: Direct Object

A **direct object** is a noun or pronoun that receives the action of the verb. Find the direct object in a sentence by asking *Whom?* or *What?* about the verb.

> Mr. Suzuki bought *a new computer.*
> > Bought what? *a new computer*
>
> The police helped *the frightened woman.*
> > Helped whom? *the frightened woman*
>
> Alexi mailed *the package* to her sister.
> > Mailed what? *the package*

**Identify It**

Underline the verb in each sentence below. Then, circle the direct object.

1. The members of the hockey team signed autographs for their fans.

2. The forward shot the puck across the rink.

3. The referee called a penalty.

4. The goalie quickly blocked the puck.

5. Sam bought a hockey jersey with Wayne Gretzky's name on it.

6. The referee gave a penalty shot to a player on the other team.

7. Angela Ruggiero and Kristin King play hockey for the U.S. National Team.

8. The Toronto Aeros beat the Montreal Axion in the 2005 NWHL Championship.

NAME _____

## Lesson 1.15  Parts of a Sentence: Direct Object

**Identify It**

Read each sentence below. If the underlined words are the direct object, make a check mark on the line. If they are not the direct object, make an **X** on the line. Then, find the correct direct object and circle it.

1. _____ I saw <u>my first hockey game</u> yesterday.

2. _____ Uncle Gil and <u>my cousin Cristina</u> took me.

3. _____ Hundreds of people filled <u>the arena</u>.

4. _____ Uncle Gil explained <u>each play</u> to me.

5. _____ During the game, <u>the puck</u> hit the dividing glass at an incredible speed.

6. _____ It startled <u>me</u>, and I jumped!

7. _____ Cristina <u>shot</u> some photographs of her favorite players.

8. _____ Cristina plays roller hockey <u>with some kids from her school.</u>

**Try It**

Write three sentences on the lines below. Make sure each sentence has a direct object.

1. _____

2. _____

3. _____

## Review Parts of a Sentence

The **subject** of a sentence is what a sentence is about.
> *The highest mountain in North America* is in Denali National Park.
> *Grandma Ruth* likes to garden and play tennis.

To find the subject in a question, ask yourself who or what the sentence is about. Double-check your answer by turning the sentence into a statement.
> Will *Gabrielle* ride her bike or walk?
> *Gabrielle* will ride her bike or walk.

In a command, the subject is "understood *you*."
> Use scrap paper for the art project.
> (*You*) use scrap paper for the art project.

A **predicate** tells what the subject of a sentence is or does. The predicate includes the verb.
> The chestnut horse *grazes in the meadow*.
> Mr. Vogel *planted a butterfly garden*.

A **direct object** is a noun or pronoun that receives the action of the verb. Find the direct object in a sentence by asking *Whom?* or *What?* about the verb.
> Nathan takes *tae kwon do*.    Takes what? *tae kwon do*
> Elizabeth sent *an e-mail* to Habib.    Sent what? *an e-mail*

### Putting It Together

In each sentence, underline the subject once and the predicate twice.

1. Lynne Cox is a long-distance ocean swimmer.

2. She set records for swimming the Catalina Channel and the English Channel.

3. Doctors and scientists can't explain her achievements.

4. Can you imagine swimming in 33°F water?

## Review Parts of a Sentence

Read the sentences below. If the underlined phrase is the subject, write **S** on the line. If it is a predicate, write **P**. If it is a direct object, write **DO**.

1. _____ Lynne Cox began <u>her open-water swims</u> as a child.

2. _____ As a teenager, she <u>swam California's Catalina Channel</u>.

3. _____ She swam <u>21 miles</u> in about 12 hours.

4. _____ <u>Lynne</u> swam from Alaska to the Soviet Union in 1987.

5. _____ This <u>happened during the Cold War</u>.

6. _____ <u>America and the Soviet Union</u> did not have good relations.

7. _____ Lynne's swim helped <u>the two countries</u> begin to form a bond.

8. _____ <u>(You)</u> Read more about Lynne at her Web site, www.lynnecox.org.

In each sentence below, circle the verb. Then, draw an arrow from the verb to the direct object.

1. In 2002, Lynne swam a mile in the waters of Antarctica.

2. She saw icebergs during her swim.

3. It took 25 minutes to complete.

4. Most people can't survive such cold temperatures.

5. Lynne has trained her body to adjust.

6. Her blood keeps her important organs warm.

# Lesson 1.16 Sentence Fragments

A sentence is a group of words that contains a complete thought and has a subject and a predicate. A **sentence fragment** is part of a sentence, or an incomplete sentence. A sentence fragment may be a subject, a predicate, or just a few words grouped together. Sentence fragments cannot stand alone.

| Sentence Fragment: | Sentence: |
| --- | --- |
| *Played the piano.* | *Joe played the piano.* |
| *In the morning.* | *In the morning, Sara ran two miles.* |

## Identify It

Read each item below. If it is a complete sentence, write **C** on the line. If it is a sentence fragment, write an **F** on the line.

1. _____ Painted an underwater scene on the walls of the room.

2. _____ After Leo and Nina moved the furniture.

3. _____ Grandpa watered the plants.

4. _____ The ladybug climbed onto the leaf.

5. _____ Rained for four days.

6. _____ The boys and their teacher.

7. _____ The biologist peered through his microscope.

8. _____ Put the books in a paper bag and carried them to the car.

9. _____ Mom goes bowling on Tuesdays.

## Lesson 1.16 Sentence Fragments

**Rewrite It**

Read the sentence fragments below. Add words to each fragment to form a complete sentence. Write the sentences on the lines. Do not forget to use capital letters and end marks where they are needed.

1. went to the movies on Saturday afternoon

   _____

2. always enjoys movies about

   _____

3. the theater was full, but some seats

   _____

4. the funniest part of the movie

   _____

5. ordered a bucket of popcorn to share

   _____

6. I think that the best movies

   _____

**Try It**

Write three sentence fragments on a separate sheet of paper. On the lines below, write your fragments as complete sentences.

1. _____

2. _____

3. _____

## Lesson 1.17 Compound Sentences

A **compound sentence** contains two or more complete sentences. The sentences are joined by a comma and a conjunction like *and, or,* or *but.*

The children went swimming, *and* the adults talked for hours.

We will go to the car show, *or* we will go shopping.

Raphael went to the market, *but* they were out of tomatoes.

A sentence that has two subjects or two verbs is not always a compound sentence. Remember, there must be two complete subjects and predicates to form a compound.

(subject)     (predicate)          (predicate)

Simple: *Sammy put on his uniform* and *walked down the stairs.*

(subject)    (predicate)    (subject)    (predicate)

Compound: *Sammy put on a hat,* and *he walked down the stairs.*

**Identify It**

Read the diary entry below. Underline the four compound sentences.

Dear Diary,

    Last weekend, I visited my aunt and uncle. They live in a house in the country, but it isn't a real farm. The only animals they have are barn cats and a sheepdog, but they do own five acres of land.

    Uncle Spencer and I decided to go exploring. We packed a lunch and headed across the big field behind his house. We walked for about an hour, and I spotted several deer and a turkey. Uncle Spencer and I found a great spot for lunch.

    After lunch, we decided to poke around some more and see what we could find. My uncle found a brick with the year 1888 on it. I found the top of an old desk.

    "I think this is an old schoolhouse!" exclaimed Uncle Spencer. "Let's do some research, and we'll find out for sure."

## Lesson 1.17 Compound Sentences

### Complete It

Read each sentence below. If it is a compound sentence, make a check mark on the line. If it is not a compound sentence, make an **X** on the line. Then, add words to the sentence to turn it into a compound.

> ^ – **insert words**

Example: __X__ I looked out the window∧and∧could see for miles.

1. _____ My uncle found part of a chalkboard, and I found a book.

2. _____ The words were faded, but I could almost read them.

3. _____ I wondered whose book it had been and when someone had last used it.

4. _____ I picked up the chalkboard and showed it to Uncle Spencer.

5. _____ I wished there was writing on it, but decades of weather had washed everything clean.

6. _____ Uncle Spencer tripped over something and crouched down to see what it was.

7. _____ He had discovered a rusty school bell and shook off the damp leaves to get a better look.

8. _____ I loved the mystery of digging up a little piece of the past and couldn't wait to learn more about what we had found.

### Try It

What do you think happens next to Uncle Spencer and his nephew? Write a sentence that continues the story.

_____

## Lesson 1.18  Run-On Sentences

**Run-on sentences** are sentences that are too long or contain too much information. Sometimes, adding a comma and a conjunction like *and, or,* or *but* will fix the run-on. Other times, the run-on sentence must be split into two separate sentences or rewritten.

In the examples that follow, the first sentence is a run-on. The next two sentences show different ways to fix a run-on sentence.

<u>Run-on:</u> Darcy speaks Spanish her friend Logan speaks French.

Darcy speaks Spanish**,** *and* her friend Logan speaks French.

Darcy speaks Spanish**.** Her friend Logan speaks French.

### Identify It

Read each sentence below. If it is a complete sentence, make a check mark on the line. If it is a run-on sentence, write **RO** on the line. Then, make a slash (/) where you would divide the sentence.

1. _____ Wolves don't have a very good reputation.

2. _____ Do you remember the story of Little Red Riding Hood or the Three Little Pigs?

3. _____ Some people are frightened by these wild creatures they believe that wolves attack easily.

4. _____ Wolves are shy around humans they would prefer not to be seen.

5. _____ In the American West, wolves hunt animals like deer and rabbits.

6. _____ They can be a problem for farmers they sometimes attack sheep or cattle.

7. _____ A wolf's coat is thick and beautiful it is made of two layers of fur.

8. _____ The top layer keeps away water and dirt the bottom layer keeps the animal warm.

## Lesson 1.18 Run-On Sentences

**Proof It**

Read the run-on sentences below. Correct each sentence using proofreading marks. You may need to add a comma and a conjunction, or you may need to divide it into two sentences. If you make two separate sentences, remember to capitalize the first word of the new sentence.

> ∧ – **inserts words and punctuation**
> ≡ – **capitalizes a letter**

1. Wolves are related to dogs their paws, legs, and jaws are stronger.

2. Wolves live and travel in packs there are usually between two and six wolves in a pack.

3. A pack is usually led by a male and a female they are the alpha wolves.

4. Alpha wolves have the highest rank in a pack they have the most freedom.

5. Wolves in the wild live six to nine years they can live about twice as long in captivity.

6. People who visit Yellowstone Park often see wolves the wolves don't usually come too close.

**Try It**

Write two run-on sentences on a separate sheet of paper about an animal that you find interesting. On the lines below, correct your run-on sentences.

1. _____

2. _____

 # Sentence Fragments, Compound Sentences, and Run-On Sentences

A **sentence fragment** is part of a sentence, or an incomplete sentence. Sentence fragments cannot stand alone.

> Sentence Fragment: *During the show*
> Sentence: *During the show, Joe played the piano.*

A **compound sentence** contains two or more complete sentences. The sentences are joined by a comma and a conjunction like *and, or,* or *but.*

> Shannon made a collage**,** *and* Kahlil drew a picture.

**Run-on sentences** are sentences that are too long or contain too much information. Adding a comma and a conjunction can make a compound sentence. It can also be split into two separate, complete sentences.

> Bamboo is the fastest growing plant͟. ͟S͟ome species can grow about a foot in a day. Most bamboo grows in East and Southeast Asia, ͵but ͵it also grows in other tropical climates.

## Putting It Together

Read each item below. If it is a fragment, write **F** on the line. If it is a run-on sentence, write **RO** on the line. If it is a compound sentence, write **C** on the line.

1. _____ The word *piano* comes from the Italian word *pianoforte* it means *soft-loud.*

2. _____ Bartolomeo Cristofori invented the piano, but no one is sure of the exact date.

3. _____ Two of his pianos, from the 1720s.

4. _____ Similar to the clavichord and harpsichord.

5. _____ The keys move felt-covered hammers, and the hammers cause the strings to vibrate and create sound.

# Review Sentence Fragments, Compound Sentences, and Run-On Sentences

Read the paragraph below. Underline the three compound sentences. Then, find the three run-on sentences. Use proofreading marks to correct them.

| | |
|---|---|
| ∧ | – inserts words and punctuation |
| ≡ | – capitalizes a letter |

A modern piano has 88 keys it covers a range of more than seven octaves. Some older pianos have fewer keys. Others have an extra set of keys they are hidden under a small lid. Today, there are two main types of pianos. The grand piano is about six to nine feet long, and it sounds best when played in a room with high ceilings. Concert grand pianos are usually used for public shows because longer pianos often have better sound. Upright pianos have vertical strings, and grand pianos have horizontal strings. Vertical pianos don't take up as much space grand pianos are more sensitive to the player's touch.

Add words to each sentence fragment to form a complete sentence. Write the sentences on the lines. Do not forget to use capital letters and end marks where they are needed.

1. plays the piano

   _____

2. takes lessons once a week

   _____

3. the teacher, Mr. Valentine,

   _____

**Lesson 1.19** # Combining Sentences: Subjects and Direct Objects

**Combining sentences** can help a writer avoid repeating words. It can also make the writing read more smoothly. If two sentences tell about the same thing, they can be combined. If the subject of the sentence changes from singular to plural (or vice-versa), remember to change the verb so that it agrees.

Combining Subjects:

*Olivia* lives on 42nd Street. *Natalie* lives on 42nd Street.

*Olivia and Natalie* live on 42nd Street.

Combining Direct Objects:

Takumi ate *a turkey sandwich*. Takumi ate *a crisp, green apple*.

Takumi ate *a turkey sandwich and a crisp, green apple*.

## Identify It

Read each set of sentences below. If the sentences can be combined, make a check mark on the line. If they tell about different things and cannot be combined, make an **X** on the line.

1. _____ The Big Dipper is a well-known constellation. Orion is a well-known constellation.

2. _____ Alisha used her telescope to see Aquarius. Alisha used her telescope to see Pegasus.

3. _____ Groups of stars may be named after animals or objects. Some are named after heroes of mythology.

4. _____ Some constellations can be seen only from the Northern Hemisphere. Other constellations can be seen only from the Southern Hemisphere.

5. _____ You can see Andromeda in the winter sky. You can see Cygnus, the swan, in the summer and fall.

# Lesson 1.19 Combining Sentences: Subjects and Direct Objects

**Rewrite It**

Combine each pair of sentences below into one sentence. Write the new sentence on the line.

1. Jasmine used the telescope at the observatory. Aaron used the telescope at the observatory.

   _____

2. Aaron knows a lot about stars. Jasmine is knowledgeable about stars, too.

   _____

3. In Greek mythology, Cassiopeia was a queen. In Greek mythology, Cassiopeia was Andromeda's mother.

   _____

4. Cassiopeia can be seen all year in the Northern Hemisphere. Ursa Major and Ursa Minor can be seen all year, too.

   _____

5. Scorpius and Orion are enemies. Scorpius and Orion are visible in different seasons.

   _____

6. You can learn more about constellations online. You can also learn more about constellations in books of Greek mythology.

   _____

## Lesson 1.20  Combining Sentence: Verbs

When two or more sentences tell about the same thing, they can sometimes be combined using the words *and* or *or*. If you list several things in a row, remember to place a comma after each one.

> Ryan might go for a bike ride. He might play soccer. He might go to a movie.

> Ryan might go for a bike ride, play soccer, *or* go to a movie.

**Complete It**

Read the sentences below. Fill in each blank with a comma or the missing word or words.

1. Isabel looked at the recipes in her cookbook. She checked the cupboards for ingredients.

   Isabel _____ at the recipes in her cookbook and _____ the cupboards for ingredients.

2. Isabel and Simon might make oatmeal-banana bread. They might bake oatmeal-raisin cookies.

   _____ might make oatmeal-banana bread__ or _____ might bake oatmeal-raisin cookies.

3. Isabel likes raisins better than bananas. She decided to make oatmeal-raisin cookies.

   Isabel _____ raisins better than bananas and _____ to make oatmeal-raisin cookies.

4. Isabel and Simon measured the sugar. They added some vanilla. They cracked the eggs.

   Isabel and Simon measured the sugar__ added some vanilla__ _____ cracked the eggs.

## Lesson 1.20  Combining Sentence: Verbs

**Rewrite It**

Combine each set of sentences below into one
sentence. Write the new sentence on the line.

1. Isabel plugged in the mixer. She beat the
   sugar, butter, eggs, and vanilla.

   _____

2. Simon added the flour. He poured in the oats. He blended the
   ingredients.

   _____

3. Simon sprinkled raisins on top of the mixture. Simon stirred the dough.

   _____

4. Isabel and Simon scooped up spoonfuls of cookie dough. They
   dropped them onto the cookie sheet.

   _____

5. The two friends cleaned up the kitchen. The two friends waited for the
   cookies to bake.

   _____

6. They might bring the cookies to school. They might save them for a
   picnic on Saturday.

   _____

7. Isabel's mom heard the kitchen timer ring. Isabel's mom took the
   cookies out of the oven.

   _____

NAME _____

## Lesson 1.21 Combining Sentences: Adjectives

Sentences that use adjectives to describe the same thing can often be combined. In the sentences that follow, the adjectives *blue, heavy,* and *rectangular* all describe *box*. Remember to use commas after each item in a series, except the last.

> Liam carried the *blue* box up the stairs. The box was *rectangular* and heavy.
>
> Liam carried the *heavy, rectangular, blue* box up the stairs.
>
> The spelling bee contestants were *young*. They felt *excited*. They were also *nervous*.
>
> The *young* spelling bee contestants were *excited* and *nervous*.

**Identify It**

There are three pairs of sentences that can be combined in the paragraphs below. Underline each pair.

The Metropolitan Museum of Art is a large museum. It is an important museum. Many people call it "The Met." It is located near Central Park in New York City. The collection of artworks is valuable. It is impressive. There are nearly three million objects housed at the museum. It would take about five and a half years to look at everything if you spent one minute per object.

Some displays and events are just for children. If you have a chance to visit the museum, you should be sure to see the Egyptian Temple of Dendur. The temple was brought to America from Egypt by ship. The temple is more than 2,000 years old. The temple is very popular with tourists.

## Lesson 1.21 Combining Sentences: Adjectives

**Rewrite It**

Combine each set of sentences below into a single sentence. Write the new sentence on the line.

1. The enormous painting hanging in the hall was bright. It was colorful.

   _____

2. Vicente touched the stone sculpture of a bird. It felt smooth. It felt cold.

   _____

3. The collage made by the fourth-grade class was interesting. The collage was unusual.

   _____

4. The print hanging in the gallery was made with vegetable dyes. The print was beautiful.

   _____

5. The ancient carving was tiny and intricate. It was wooden.

   _____

**Try It**

1. Write two sentences that describe an object you might see in a museum. Use a different adjective in each sentence.

   _____

   _____

2. Now, write a sentence that combines the two sentences you wrote.

   _____

## Review | Combining Sentences

Two or more sentences that tell about the same thing can sometimes be combined. **Combining sentences** helps a writer avoid repeating words. It makes the writing smoother and easier to read. Commas and the words *and* and *or* are often used to combine sentences.

When you combine sentences, make sure that the subject and verb agree in the new sentence you create.

Combining subjects:

Jordan's grandma was born in the 1940s. Brian's grandpa was born in the 1940s.

*Jordan's grandma and Brian's grandpa* were born in the 1940s.

Combining direct objects:

Mr. Blumberg vacuumed the living room. He vacuumed the dining room.

Mr. Blumberg vacuumed *the living room and the dining room*.

Combining verbs:

The tree branch swayed during the storm. Then, it cracked. The branch fell to the ground.

The tree branch swayed during the storm, cracked, *and* fell to the ground.

Combining adjectives:

We watched the sunset from the dock. The sunset was breathtaking. It was fiery.

We watched the *breathtaking, fiery* sunset from the dock.

## Review Combining Sentences

**Putting It Together**

Combine each set of sentences below into a single sentence. Write the new sentence on the line.

1. The Amazon rain forest is located in South America. It is the largest rain forest in the world.

   _____

2. Tropical rain forests are hot. They are moist. Rain forests are lush.

   _____

3. Some species of insects are unique to the rain forests. Some animals are unique to the rain forests.

   _____

4. Most rain forest insects live high in the canopy. Most rain forest insects are beetles.

   _____

There are three pairs of sentences that can be combined in the paragraphs below. Underline each pair.

The animals of the rain forest interest scientists. The animals of the rain forest are fascinating. Scientists have identified some species but know little about them. Other species have yet to be discovered.

In the space of only a few miles, more than 100 types of mammals can be found. Some rain forest animals live on the ground. Many spend a good deal of time in the canopy. The canopy is high above the forest floor. The plants and animals in a rain forest often depend on each other. They may use one another for food, protection, shelter, and pollination.

# Chapter 2
## Lesson 2.1 Capitalizing Names and Titles

Capitalize the **names of specific people and pets**.

      **S**ally named the kittens **C**laudia, **C**lemson, **C**arter, and **C**amille.

      **J**ane **G**oodall studies chimpanzees.

A **title** gives more information about who a person is. **Titles that come before a name** and **titles of respect** are capitalized.

| | | |
|---|---|---|
| **G**randma **P**earl | **U**ncle **S**antos | **M**ayor **D**evlin |
| **O**fficer **B**ernhardt | **N**urse **C**apshaw | **J**udge **M**ay **B**ennett |
| **M**s. **C**houdhry | **D**r. **R**ozic | **M**r. **Z**hu |

If a title is not used with a name, it is not capitalized.

      My *grandpa* collects Civil War uniforms.

      The *nurse* gave me a bandage.

But if a title is used as a name, it is capitalized.

      On Sunday, **G**randpa made scrambled eggs.

      Will **M**om pick us up today?

## Complete It

Read the sentences below. Underline the word in parentheses that correctly completes each sentence and write it on the line.

1. On Friday afternoon, I have an appointment with _____ Ali. (dr., Dr.)

2. My _____ lives in an apartment above a pet store. (Aunt, aunt)

3. Ana is going to interview her grandpa, who was a _____ for 42 years. (Judge, judge)

4. Our neighbors got a chinchilla and named it _____. (harriet, Harriet)

5. Which game did you and your _____ play? (dad, Dad)

6. Lindsay's uncle is _____ O'Hara. (Captain, captain)

NAME _____

## Lesson 2.1  Capitalizing Names and Titles

**Proof It**

Read the diary entry below. Use proofreading marks to correct the 11 mistakes in capitalization.

| ☰ – capitalize a letter |
| / – lowercase a letter |

Dear Diary,

    I have been researching my family tree. I have learned many interesting things about my relatives. For example, grandma Helen was a trapeze artist. She did a show with an elephant named farley. Mom also told me that uncle thomas was a famous author in the early 1900s. He wrote more than 20 books. I even found out that I am a distant Cousin of president Hoover!

    Mayor Glass is the Mayor of the town where mom's family lived. I have e-mailed her for information from the town's records. I want to learn about a woman named rose amelia saxon. I was named after her, but I don't know anything about her life.

**Try It**

1. Write the names of three people you know who have titles before their names.

_____

2. Think of two people you know who have pets. Write their names below.

Person:_____     Pet:_____

Person:_____     Pet:_____

Spectrum Language Arts
Grade 4

Chapter 2 Lesson 1
Mechanics: Capitalization

63

## Lesson 2.2  Capitalizing Place Names

The **names of specific places** always begin with a capital letter.

| | |
|---|---|
| Appalachian Mountains | Baltimore, Maryland |
| India | Colgate University |
| Lakewood Little Theater | Portland Art Museum |

**Complete It**

Answer each question below using a complete sentence. Remember to capitalize the names of specific places.

1. What school do you attend?

   _____

2. If you could visit any country in the world, where would you go?

   _____

3. In what city and state do you live?

   _____

4. Which planet would you most like to visit? Why?

   _____

5. Name a museum, zoo, park, or library you have visited.

   _____

**Tip**

- The names of the planets begin with a capital letter.
- When *Earth* refers to the planet, capitalize it. When it refers to the soil or ground, lowercase it.
  The third planet from the sun is *Earth*.
  The *earth* in this area is rich with nutrients.

## Lesson 2.2 Capitalizing Place Names

**Proof It**

Read the brochure below. There are 21 mistakes in capitalization. Use proofreading marks to correct the errors.

≡ - capitalize a letter
/ - lowercase a letter

Example: The wettest place in the United States is m̲ount w̲aialeale in the
         S̸tate of Hawaii.

---

Welcome to Miami, florida, where the Sun is always shining!

We are glad you have decided to make our beautiful City your home!
We are located on the miami river, between the Everglades and the atlantic Ocean.
We are a diverse city with many citizens from Latin America, the caribbean, and europe.

Once you are settled in your new Home, it will be time to do some exploring. The following attractions are fun for all newcomers—old and young alike.

- Coconut Grove
- the Miami art museum
- the miami seaquarium
- Parrot Jungle Island
- Little Havana
- the fairchild Tropical Gardens

Also, be sure to visit the Miami-Dade public library on west flagler Street, Bicentennial park on Biscayne boulevard, and the farmers' market at the corner of Miami Avenue and Flagler street.

---

**Try It**

Imagine that someone has just moved to your hometown from another state. Write a short paragraph telling them about some places they could visit. Use at least four specific place names in your paragraph.

_____

_____

_____

_____

## Lesson 2.3  Capitalizing Dates and Holidays

The **days of the week** each begin with a capital letter.

> Sunday, Monday, Tuesday, Wednesday, Thursday, Friday, Saturday

The **months** of the year are capitalized.

> January, February, March, April, May, June, July,
> August, September, October, November, December

The **names of holidays** are capitalized.

> Earth Day     Father's Day     New Year's Eve     Memorial Day

### Complete It

Fill in the blanks below with the words in parentheses. Use capital letters when needed.

1. Theodore's favorite holiday is _____. (thanksgiving)

2. Veronica prefers _____. (valentine's day)

3. Felix and Franny were both born on an icy _____ in _____. (friday/february)

4. _____ is a very busy month for Andre and Angelina. (august)

5. On _____, Mr. Victor Vega has a reunion with soldiers from his platoon. (veteran's day)

6. In _____, Sanjana will travel to Syria, Singapore, Sweden, and Sicily. (september)

7. Maureen meets Morgan for lunch every _____. (monday)

8. Greg will travel to Punxsutawney, Pennsylvania for _____. (groundhog's day)

# Lesson 2.3 Capitalizing Dates and Holidays

## Rewrite It

Rewrite each sentence below using capital letters for dates and holidays.

1. mother's day always falls on the second sunday in may.

   _____

2. China and Vietnam do not celebrate new year's day on january 1.

   _____

3. rosh hashanah and yom kippur are Jewish holidays celebrated in september.

   _____

   _____

4. The fourth thursday in november is thanksgiving.

   _____

5. kwanzaa is a holiday that begins on december 26 and celebrates the goodness of life.

   _____

   _____

6. independence day has been celebrated on july 4 since 1777.

   _____

## Try It

1. Write the month and year you were born on the line below.

   _____

2. Write the name of the holiday that is closest to your birthday.

   _____

# Lesson 2.4   Capitalizing Book, Movie, and Song Titles

The **titles of books, movies, and songs** are capitalized. Do not capitalize prepositions, articles, or conjunctions, like *of, the, and, in, to, a, an,* and *from,* unless they are the first or last word of a title.

| **Books** | **Movies** | **Songs** |
|---|---|---|
| <u>Because of Winn-Dixie</u> | <u>The Incredibles</u> | "Here Comes the Sun" |
| <u>Tuck Everlasting</u> | <u>The Polar Express</u> | "Getting to Know You" |
| <u>A Long Way from Chicago</u> | <u>Harriet the Spy</u> | "At the Bottom of the Sea" |

## Complete It

Fill the blanks below with the titles of books, movies, or songs. Use capital letters where they are needed. Remember to underline book and movie titles. Use quotation marks with song titles.

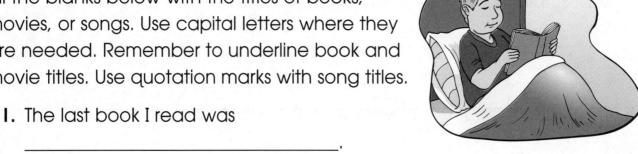

1. The last book I read was

   _____.

2. If I were a movie critic, I would *not* give a "thumbs-up" to

   _____.

3. One of my favorite songs when I was little was

   _____.

4. I would recommend the book _____.

5. I know all the words to the song _____.

6. The best movie I've seen this year is _____.

7. I like the book _____ because the characters seem like real people.

8. I laughed incredibly hard when I saw the movie

   _____.

## Lesson 2.4 Capitalizing Book, Movie, and Song Titles

**Proof It**

Read the letter below. There are 14 mistakes in capitalization. Use proofreading marks to correct the mistakes.

| ≡ – capitalize a letter |
| / – lowercase a letter |

February 23

Dear Kyle,

How's life in Texas? It's time for our monthly book and movie review. I read <u>tales Of A Fourth Grade nothing</u> last week, and I thought it was hilarious. The main character has a pesky younger brother, so I know you could relate to it. <u>dolphin treasure</u> by Wayne Grover is a great adventure. If you are in the mood for a mystery, I would highly recommend <u>the Canoe Trip mystery</u>.

I finally saw the movie <u>holes</u>. It is as good as the book, and I guarantee that you will not be disappointed. When you have a chance, you should also see <u>spy kids</u> and <u>Robots</u>.

It's time for me to wrap this up. I have a big pile of homework to do. Serena has been listening to our parents' oldies CD all afternoon. I am really tired of hearing "Splish Splash," "rockin' robin," and "lollipop"!

Your favorite cousin,

Micah

**Try It**

Imagine that you published a book, wrote a song, and directed a movie. What would you name your creations? Write the titles on the lines below.

_____

_____

NAME _____

## Review Capitalization

Capitalize the names of **specific people and pets**.

    My sister, **N**ikki, wrote a story about a pet monkey named **S**quizzle.

Capitalize **titles that come before a name**.

    **A**unt Linh   **S**enator Rivera   **M**rs. Wasserbauer   **D**r. Oakley

Do not capitalize titles that are used alone, unless they are used as a name.

    My *dad* plays basketball.    I asked *Dad* to close the windows.

Capitalize the **names of specific places**.

    **L**inden **H**ospital   **Q**uincy, **M**assachusetts   **G**rady **P**reschool   **B**razil

The **days of the week** and **months of the year** begin with a capital letter.

    **T**uesday, **F**riday, **S**unday       **A**pril, **J**une, **O**ctober, **D**ecember

The names of holidays are capitalized.

    **P**resident's **D**ay   **I**ndependence **D**ay   **M**other's **D**ay

The **titles of books, movies, and songs** are capitalized. Do not capitalize prepositions, articles, or conjunctions unless they are the first or last word of a title.

    Barbara Park wrote <u>**T**he **K**id in the **R**ed **J**acket</u>.

**Putting It Together**

Complete each sentence below with the words in parentheses. Some of the words will need to be capitalized, and others will not.

1. My _____ (grandpa) and his dog, _____ (callie), are coming to see our new house.

2. They are coming on _____ (friday) morning and staying through _____ (labor day).

3. I gave _____ (grandpa) directions from his office on _____ (wellspring street).

4. "Our house is a mile past _____ (dr. twombly's) office on _____ (carter avenue)," I said.

Spectrum Language Arts
Grade 4
70

Review: Chapter 2 Lessons 1-4
Mechanics: Capitalization

# Review Capitalization

There are 17 mistakes in capitalization in the datebook entries below. Correct the mistakes using proofreading marks.

≡ – capitalize a letter
/ – lowercase a letter

## Dates to Remember

february 14    valentine's day party

March 3        Take Milo and roxy to the vet at 3:30

March 8        uncle Tommy's flight from chile arrives at 6:30

March 12       Birthday party for Katie Wang—1426 East willow drive

March 19       Order The Wind In The Willows and charlotte's web for

               brighton School book drive

March 30       Hailey's appointment with dr. Traynor at 4:15

april 9        Free tickets at clover Children's Museum, friday–Sunday

Rewrite the sentences below using capital letters where needed.

1. beverly cleary wrote <u>ralph s. mouse</u> and <u>ramona and her mother</u>.

   _____

2. officer gomez lives and works in santa ana, california.

   _____

3. on father's day, we rented the movies <u>hook</u> and <u>a bug's life</u>.

   _____

4. julie andrews sang "spoonful of sugar" in the movie <u>mary poppins</u>.

   _____

## Lesson 2.5 Periods

A **period** is an end mark that follows a statement or a command. Use a period to end a declarative or an imperative sentence.

> Washington borders Oregon and Idaho.   Put the marbles in the jar.

Periods also follow **abbreviations**. Use a period after an **initial**, or letter that stands for a name.

> E. B. White          George W. Bush          Danielle A. Williams

**People's titles** are usually abbreviated when they come before a name.

> Mrs. = Mistress          Mr. = Mister          Dr. = Doctor

The **days of the week** and the **months of the year** are often abbreviated.

> Fri. afternoon     Oct. 28, 1988    Mon.–Thurs.    Jan. 15

**Types of streets** are abbreviated in addresses.

> Caroline Blvd.          Rockingham Rd.          Huckleberry Ave.

**Measurements** can also be abbreviated.

> in. = inch       ft. = feet       yd. = yard     mi. = mile     oz. = ounce
> pt. = pint       qt. = quart     gal. = gallon  lb. = pound   c. = cup

### Rewrite It

Read each sentence below. Then, rewrite the bold words using an abbreviation.

1. Robbie is 4 **feet** _____ 11 **inches** _____ tall.

2. The Hughes family is moving to Redwing **Court** _____.

3. Mom bought a **pint** _____ of blueberries and a **quart** _____ of strawberries.

4. Vikram's birthday is **Thursday** _____, **August** _____ 8.

5. **Alan Alexander** _____ Milne is the author of the Winnie the Pooh books.

## Lesson 2.5  Periods

**Proof It**

Read the brochure below. It is missing 18 periods. Add the periods where they are needed. Remember to circle them so that they are easy to see.

### Time to take a dip at Valley Ridge Pool!

Valley Ridge Pool will be open for the summer from Mon., May 30–Sat , Sept 2

Join us for swimming lessons, lap swim, water aerobics, and synchronized swimming

Our low dive is 4 ft tall The high dive is 16 ft tall

We have a snack bar, a kiddie pool, showers, and a 30-yd pool

Children under 3 ft tall must be accompanied by an adult

Pool Manager: Mr. J P. Stevens

Lifeguards: Cassidy L Wickline, Grace Yamamoto, P Ellis Snyder

Pool Hours: Mon–Sat.: 9 a.m. until 7 p.m. Sun.: noon until 6 p.m.

Location: the corner of Cherry Ln and Bellhaven St

**Try It**

Interview a friend. Write your friend's answers on the lines below using abbreviations as often as possible.

What is your complete name?  _____

What is your address? _____

How tall are you? _____

When is your birthday? _____

# Lesson 2.6  Question Marks and Exclamation Points

Use a **question mark** to end a sentence that asks a question.

>Did you put away the milk**?**

>What type of currency do people use in Japan**?**

Use an **exclamation point** to end a sentence that expresses strong feelings, like excitement, happiness, surprise, anger, and fear.

>Don't take that bicycle**!**        My computer crashed**!**

## Complete It

Read the interview below. Some sentences are missing end marks. Complete the sentences with a question mark or an exclamation point.

**Mateo:** How did you first become interested in reptiles?

**Mr. O'Toole:** I've been interested since I was a small boy. I caught my first lizard when I was only two__

**Mateo:** Where have your travels taken you__

**Mr. O'Toole:** I've visited many fascinating countries, like Brazil, Thailand, and Australia. I have traveled all the way around the world three times!

**Mateo:** Wow__ That's incredible__

**Mr. O'Toole:** Are you interested in traveling, Mateo__

**Mateo:** Yes, I'd love to see the world one day. Which expedition was your favorite__

**Mr. O'Toole:** Borneo is at the top of my list. I had some interesting experiences with unusual reptiles there.

**Mateo:** Did you ever feel like you were in serious danger __

**Mr. O'Toole:** More times than I can count__ It's just part of the job.

## Lesson 2.6  Question Marks and Exclamation Points

**Proof It**

There are seven mistakes in punctuation in the paragraphs below. Delete incorrect end marks and add question marks or exclamation points where they are needed.

> *e* – deletes punctuation
> ∧ – inserts punctuation

Reptiles are cold-blooded animals that are covered with scales. Most reptiles hatch from eggs. Unlike amphibians, their scaly skin is not moist. It also does not let water in. There are more than 7,000 species of reptiles in the world today? How many of them are you familiar with.

Turtles are interesting creatures. A turtle's shell is a portable type of protection. The smallest turtles are only about four inches long. The largest can weigh about 2,000 pounds. Turtles also have an amazing life span. Giant tortoises can live to be 150 years old?

Have you ever heard of tuataras! Tuataras are similar to lizards. Scientists sometimes call them "living fossils." Can you guess why. This type of reptile is older than the dinosaurs. Scientists believe that tuataras may have existed for more than 225 million years? The only place they are still found today is on some islands near New Zealand.

**Try It**

On the lines below, continue the interview from page 74. End one sentence with a question mark and one with an exclamation point.

**Mateo:** _____

**Mr. O'Toole:** _____

## Review  End Marks and Abbreviations

A **period** follows a statement or a command.

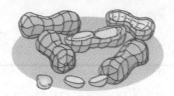

    Elizabeth Cady Stanton fought for voting rights.

    Give me the peanuts, please.

A period is used after **initials** and after people's titles.

    Franklin D. Roosevelt    T. S. Eliot    Mrs. Bell    Dr. Kovitch

The **days of the week**, **months of the year**, and **types of streets** are often abbreviated.

    Wed. morning        Dec. 4, 2004        Maple Ave.

**Measurements** are often abbreviated.

    in. = inch    ft. = feet    yd. = yard    mi. = mile    oz. = ounce

    pt. = pint    qt. = quart    gal. = gallon  lb. = pound  c. = cup

A **question mark** ends a question.

    Is Selma your cousin?

    Did you know that a group of toads is called a *knot*?

An **exclamation point** ends a sentence that expresses strong feeling.

    I forgot my homework!    Congratulations on your graduation!

**Putting It Together**

Read each item below. Write the letter of the correct abbreviation in the space.

| | | |
|---|---|---|
| 1. \_\_\_\_\_ 25 pounds | **a.** 25 lbs. | **b.** 25 poun. |
| 2. \_\_\_\_\_ Robin Hood Drive | **a.** Robin Hood Dr. | **b.** Robin Hood Drv. |
| 3. \_\_\_\_\_ Elwyn Brooks White | **a.** EB. White | **b.** E. B. White |
| 4. \_\_\_\_\_ Monday–Friday | **a.** Mon.–Fri. | **b.** Mo.–Fr. |
| 5. \_\_\_\_\_ 8-ounce glass | **a.** 8-oun. glass | **b.** 8-oz. glass |
| 6. \_\_\_\_\_ January 1, 2000 | **a.** Jan. 1, 2000 | **b.** Jnry. 1, 2000 |

## Review  End Marks and Abbreviations

Read the postcard that follows. Insert the correct punctuation marks in the spaces. You will use three periods, two question marks, and two exclamation points.

Aug___ 18, 2007

Dear Chloe,

How are you___ I am writing from Calaveras Big Trees State Park in California. I think you would really like to visit this park___ It's hard to describe how amazing the redwood trees are. The largest tree here is the Louis Agassiz tree___ It is about 250 feet tall___ Experts believe these trees could continue growing forever. The oldest sequoia redwood is believed to be 3,300 years old___ Can you imagine living through so much history___

We'll be heading home tomorrow___ Even though the trip will be long, I'm looking forward to stopping at some interesting places along the way. See you soon!

Your friend,

Noah

Read each sentence below. If the end mark is used correctly, make a check mark on the line. If you find an error, make an **X** on the line. Use proofreading marks to correct the mistakes you find.

> _e_ – **deletes punctuation**
> ^ – **inserts punctuation**

1. _____ There are 129 campsites at Calaveras Big Trees State Park?

2. _____ Look how tall that tree is?

3. _____ General Sherman, General Grant, and Empire State are the names of trees in the park.

4. _____ What city is located closest to the park!

5. _____ Redwoods can grow as much as eight feet in one season.

## Lesson 2.7 Commas with Dates, Cities, and States

**Commas** are used in **dates** in between the day of the month and the year. If the date is in the middle of a sentence, use a comma after the year, too.

June 20, 1973        August 11, 2001        January 1, 2006

Maria was born on April 5, 1999, when Bryce was a year old.

**Commas** are used in between the names of **cities and states** or **cities and countries**. When used in the middle of a sentence, put a comma after the name of the state or country, too.

Chicago, Illinois        Austin, Texas        Stockholm, Sweden

My family moved from Phoenix, Arizona, to San Diego, California.

### Rewrite It

Rewrite the sentences below. Add commas where they are needed.

1. On November 7 1885 the Canadian Pacific Railway was completed.

   _____

   _____

2. The railway runs from Montreal Quebec to Vancouver British Columbia.

   _____

   _____

3. It also has branches in U.S. cities, like Minneapolis Minnesota and Chicago Illinois.

   _____

   _____

> **Tip**
> Do not use a comma between a month and a year if a date is not used.
> Lea went to Spain in March 1999.

## Lesson 2.7   Commas with Dates, Cities, and States

### Proof It

Read the sentences below. Delete commas that are not used correctly. Use proofreading marks to add commas where they are needed.

> *e* – deletes punctuation
> ^ – inserts punctuation

1. The last spike in the railway was driven at, Craigellachie British Columbia.

2. The first transcontinental train arrived on July, 4 1886.

3. An early part of the railway connected Winnipeg, Manitoba with St. Paul Minnesota.

4. The Crowsnest Pass ran from Lethbridge Alberta to Kootenay Lake.

5. King George VI and Queen Elizabeth traveled on the Canadian Pacific Railway in May, 1939.

6. On April, 24 1955 a new luxury passenger train, *The Canadian*, began service.

7. For about 35 years, "school cars" helped teachers reach students by train in remote areas of Ontario Canada.

### Try It

1. If you were traveling across the country, which two cities would you be sure to visit? Write a complete sentence to answer the question. Include the names of the cities and the states.

_____

2. Choose a famous person you admire. Find out when and where he or she was born. On the line, write a complete sentence using the information you found.

_____

# Lesson 2.8 Commas with Introductory Words, in a Series, and with Direct Address

An **introductory word** is a word that begins a sentence and introduces it to the reader. When the following words appear at the beginning of a sentence, a comma should follow: *first, last, then, next, finally, however, yes, no,* and *well.*

> *Finally,* Roman gathered his books and headed out the door.
> *However,* no one had told the boys about the clubhouse.

A **series** is a list of words. Use a comma after each word in a series except the last word.

> *Jupiter, Saturn, and Uranus* are the three largest planets.
> Isaac packed his *books, CDs, model airplane, and clothes.*

When you address a person by name, a comma separates the name from the rest of the sentence. Use a comma only with **direct address**, or when you are writing or speaking directly to a person.

> *Laura,* did you hear the news?    Thanks for your advice, *Mr. Wen.*

## Proof It

The sentences below are missing a total of eight commas. Use proofreading marks to add commas where they are needed.

| ⌃ – inserts comma |
| --- |

1. Jess do you know how to make an omelet?

2. First you must carefully crack four eggs into a bowl.

3. Then stir in a little milk.

4. Chop up some peppers zucchini spinach and cheese.

5. Finally add all the ingredients to the skillet, and let them cook over a medium heat.

6. You give excellent instructions Jess!

# Lesson 2.8  Commas with Introductory Words, in a Series, and with Direct Address

**Rewrite It**

Read the sentences below. Some sentences are missing commas. In others, the commas are in the wrong places. Rewrite each sentence using commas only where they are needed.

1. Aunt Kat will you help me plan a surprise party for, Mom?

   _____

2. First we will need to buy invitations flowers balloons and a cake.

   _____

3. Mom likes strawberries whipped cream, and chocolate cake.

   _____

4. However we have to remember that she is allergic to nuts.

   _____

5. Can you mail the invitations by tomorrow afternoon Uncle, Tony?

   _____

**Try It**

1. Imagine that you were planning a surprise party for a friend or a family member. Using a complete sentence, list four people you would invite.

   _____

2. Write three sentences to explain how you would plan the party. Begin them with the words *first*, *next*, and *last*.

   _____

   _____

   _____

# Lesson 2.9 Commas in Compound Sentences

A **compound sentence** is made of two or more complete, simple sentences. The conjunction *and, or, but,* or *so* and a comma join the simple sentences.

> Would you like to go out for lunch, *or* have you already eaten?
> I loved the book, *but* I thought the movie was dull.
> Wisconsin is the Badger State, Minnesota is the Gopher State, *and* Oregon is the Beaver State.

## Identify It

Read each sentence below. If it is a simple sentence, write **S** on the line. If it is a compound sentence, write **C** on the line. Then, underline each simple sentence in the compound sentence.

1. _____ From 1849 to 1869, thousands of Americans traveled west on the Oregon Trail.

2. _____ The trail stretched more than 2,000 miles, and it passed through what would become six states in the American West.

3. _____ Some people traveled west to find a better life, but others were hoping to find adventure and riches.

4. _____ The first large wagon train left from Missouri and carried more than 100 people.

5. _____ Some pioneers made it all the way to Oregon City, but others chose to settle at different places along the trail.

6. _____ When the first transcontinental railroad was finished in 1869, the trail was used less often.

7. _____ Would you have been willing to make the five-month-long trip, or would you have preferred the safety of home?

# Lesson 2.9  Commas in Compound Sentences

## Proof It

Read the paragraphs below. There are five missing commas. Add commas to the compound sentences.

| ↟  - inserts comma |
|---|

On the Oregon Trail, pioneers often used rocks as landmarks. The rocks showed the travelers how far they had come and they reassured people that they hadn't strayed off course. Chimney Rock in western Nebraska is easy to spot. The peak soars more than 300 feet into the sky and it can be seen from miles away. Some travelers wrote about the rock in their journals and others made sketches of it.

Another well-known landmark is Register Cliff in Guernsey, Wyoming. Some pioneers traveling the Oregon Trail just carved their names but others chose to leave messages in the soft limestone rock for people who came after them. The carvings marked the great distance a person had traveled so they were a sign of pride and accomplishment. Today, the carvings give visitors a glimpse of history.

## Try It

Imagine that you were traveling on the Oregon Trail with your family. On the lines below, write two compound sentences that describe your experiences.

_____

_____

_____

# Review Comma Usage

**Commas** are used between the **day of the month and the year**. If the date is in the middle of a sentence, use a comma after the year, too.

> March 29, 1936          September 4, 1999          January 19, 2005
> On July 21, 1969, Neil Armstrong walked on the moon.

**Commas** are used between the names of **cities and states** or **cities and countries**. When it appears in the middle of a sentence, put a comma after the name of the state or country, too.

> Charleston, West Virginia          Boise, Idaho          Vienna, Austria
> The plane arrived in Carson City, Nevada, at 6:00.

**Commas** follow **introductory words** like *first, last, then, next, finally, however, yes, no,* and *well* at the beginning of a sentence.

> *Then,* she turned off the light and went to sleep.
> *Yes,* I had a wonderful day.

A **comma** follows each word in a **series** except the last.

> *Maggie, Cezar, and Robert* got an A+ on their science project.
> Would you like *juice, milk, pop, or lemonade?*

Use a **comma** when you **directly address a person** by name.

> Can I help you with your bags, *Mrs. Rourke?*
> *Grandpa,* I went fishing today.

Use the conjunction *and, or, but,* or *so* and a comma to join two or more simple sentences in a **compound sentence**.

> The day was sunny, *and* Emily was eager to leave for the camping trip.
> We can go to the concert at the park, *or* we can go for a bike ride.

# Review Comma Usage

## Putting It Together

The letter below is missing 15 commas. Add commas where they are needed.

> ⌃ - inserts comma

March 16 2008

Dear Amit,

My family and I decided to go to Montpelier Vermont to visit my grandpa during Spring Break. He makes his own maple syrup and he promised to show us how.

The sap began to flow a couple of weeks ago so Grandpa tapped his trees. He used to use tin pails to collect the sap but today he has rubber hoses that do the job. First grandpa boiled the sap until it was sweet and thick. Next he strained it. Finally he poured it into glass bottles. Amit you have never tasted anything so delicious! We have used Grandpa's syrup on pancakes waffles French toast and ice cream.

We will be back in Lexington Kentucky by the end of the week. I will bring you a bottle of Grandpa's fresh maple syrup.

Your friend,

Alexandra

# Lesson 2.10  Punctuating Dialogue

**Dialogue** is the exact words a person says. A set of
quotation marks is used before and after dialogue.

>"Seamus goes everywhere on his skateboard."
>"This is my sister, Holly."

If the dialogue does not end the sentence, and would normally take a
period, put a comma inside the quotation marks and a period at the end
of the sentence.

>"Seamus goes everywhere on his skateboard," said Summer.
>"This is my sister, Holly," explained Kristen.

If the dialogue ends with a question mark or an exclamation point, place
the end mark inside the quotation marks. Place a period at the end of the
entire sentence.

>"Where is the Dead Sea?" asked Rob.

If part of the sentence comes before the dialogue, put a comma after
that part of the sentence. Put the end mark inside the quotation marks.

>Anna exclaimed, "I can't believe the computer crashed again!"

## Complete It

Read the sentences below. Add the correct punctuation on each line.

1. __The school fair is next weekend, isn't it?__ asked Kate.

2. Munir replied__ __Yes, it runs from Friday night until Sunday afternoon."

3. __I can't wait to dunk Mr. Halpern in the dunking booth!__ exclaimed
   Ashley.

4. "We need some more volunteers to help run the booths__ __ said
   Munir.

5. __Is anyone interested in helping?__ he asked.

6. __Just as long as I can still run the dunking booth!__ answered Ashley.

## Lesson 2.10 Punctuating Dialogue

### Proof It

Read the paragraphs below. Some of the quotation marks, commas, and end marks are missing or are in the wrong places. Use proofreading marks to correct the mistakes.

<table>
<tr><td>𝑒 – deletes punctuation</td></tr>
<tr><td>⌃ – inserts comma</td></tr>
<tr><td>ⱴ – inserts quotations</td></tr>
</table>

"I think the fair will be a great success" said Kate. We should be able to raise a lot of money for the school library she added.

Munir nodded and said "We have twice as many activities planned for this year.

"Will there be a three-legged race and a tug-of-war"? asked Ashley,

I liked the beanbag toss and bobbing for apples" said Kate. "I won a goldfish and a T-shirt! she exclaimed

Munir smiled. "All of those activities will be a part of this year's fair," he said. "I think the best addition is the teacher's pie-eating contest. Mrs. Gabrillo and Mr. Beaumont have volunteered to bake 40 blueberry pies"!

Kate asked "If they bake them, they won't have to eat them, right"?

Munir replied, I think that was their plan!

### Try It

Write a short conversation between you and a teacher, relative, or friend. Place the quotation and punctuation marks in the correct places.

_____

_____

_____

## Lesson 2.11 Punctuating Titles

**Titles of books, movies, and plays** are usually underlined.

> Chris Rock is the voice of Marty the Zebra in the hilarious movie <u>Madagascar</u>.
> <u>The Great Brain</u> is overdue at the library.
> Stone Theater is producing <u>The Legend of Sleepy Hollow</u>.

**Titles of songs, poems, and stories** are set in quotation marks.

> Robin, Andy, and Beatriz performed the song "Monster Mash."
> I memorized the poem "Stopping by Woods on a Snowy Evening" by Robert Frost.
> Maya wrote a story called "The Unbelievable Day of Penelope P. Pepper."

| Tip | Titles of books, movies, and plays may be set in italics when they are in print. <br> Have you read the book *Beetles, Lightly Toasted*? |
| --- | --- |

### Identify It

Read each sentence below. Underline the titles of books, movies, and plays. Put quotation marks around the titles of songs, stories, and poems.

1. If you like animal movies, you will probably like Homeward Bound and The Adventures of Milo and Otis.

2. My cousin knows all the songs in the play Fiddler on the Roof.

3. At preschool, my little sister learned the song Itsy Bitsy Spider.

4. Manvel ordered Tuck Everlasting from an online bookstore.

5. Devon saw the play Aladdin and the Magic Lamp in New York.

6. John Agard wrote a poem called Catch Me a Riddle.

## Lesson 2.11  Punctuating Titles

**Rewrite It**

Rewrite each sentence below. Titles should be underlined or placed in quotation marks, as necessary.

1. Why Do Heroes Have Big Feet? is a play based on tall tales of the Midwest.

   _____

   _____

2. The Rum Tum Tugger by T. S. Eliot is my father's favorite poem.

   _____

3. My favorite story in the book A Classic Treasury of Aesop's Fables is called The City Mouse and the Country Mouse.

   _____

   _____

4. Mom rented two DVDs: Lilo and Stitch, and Ella Enchanted.

   _____

**Try It**

Answer the following questions using complete sentences.

1. What is your favorite book, and who is the author?

   _____

2. What is the funniest or most interesting poem you ever read?

   _____

## Lesson 2.12 Colons

Use a **colon between the hour and the minute** when there is a reference to a specific time. There should not be a space before or after the colon.

6:30 A.M.    7:27 P.M.    at 10:45 last night    9:00–5:00 every day

Use a **colon before a list of items**. The words before the colon must be a complete sentence. Put one space after the colon before you begin the list.

You will need the following ingredients: sugar, flour, eggs, vanilla, and butter.

The kit included these items: instructions, screws, small nails, wood glue, and four wooden shelves.

**Complete It**

Read each sentence below. If the sentence is correct, make a check mark on the line. If it is not correct, make an **X** on the line. Then, add colons where they are needed.

1. _____ Eva identified the following birds at her birdfeeder robins, blue jays, cardinals, chickadees, sparrows, tufted titmice, and woodpeckers.

2. _____ Here are the ingredients you will need to make your own ginger-soda honey, apple cider vinegar, carbonated water, and sliced fresh ginger.

3. _____ The first flight arrives at 6 15, and the next one arrives at 10 06.

4. _____ Marcus's best friends are Kevin, James, Rebekah, and Jada.

5. _____ We will need the following items to make granola oats, almonds, honey, sunflower seeds, puffed rice cereal, cinnamon, canola oil, and dried fruit.

6. _____ Kickoff is at 2:30 on Saturday afternoon.

## Lesson 2.12 Colons

**Proof It**

Read the day planner below. Some colons are used incorrectly and others are missing. Add or delete colons where necessary.

| ℓ | – deletes punctuation |
| ^ | – inserts colon |

| Week of March 7–13 | |
|---|---|
| Monday, March 7 | Doctor appointment at: 2 15 |
| Tuesday, March 8 | Meeting with Mrs. Klum 4 00–4 45 |
| Wednesday, March 9 | Stop at the grocery store for: milk, wheat bread, Swiss cheese, cereal, and oranges. |
| Thursday, March 10 | Send invitations to the following families the Kobelts, the O'Malleys, and the Jiangs. |
| Friday, March 11 | Call the following businesses: to see if they will donate to the school auction Blendon's Bakery, Booktown, and Harris Market. |
| Saturday, March 12 | Cameron's soccer game at: 12 30 |
| Sunday, March 13 | Free kids' concert at McGregor Park 1 00–3 00 |

**Try It**

Use a colon and a complete sentence in your answer to each question.

1. What are three ingredients needed to make your favorite dinner?

   _____

2. Imagine that you are going on a camping trip. What are four things you would need to bring with you?

   _____

# Review Dialogue, Titles, and Colons

**Quotation marks** are used before and after **dialogue**, or the exact words a person says. If the dialogue does not end the sentence, but would normally take a period, put a comma inside the quotation marks and a period at the end of the sentence.

"I have a dream today," said Dr. King in his famous speech.

If the dialogue ends with a question mark or an exclamation point, place the end mark inside the quotation marks. Place a period at the end of the entire sentence.

"Who invented chewing gum?" asked Ian.

If part of the sentence comes before the dialogue, put a comma after that part of the sentence. Put the end mark inside the quotation marks.

Natasha asked, "What time will the bus arrive?"

**Titles of books, movies, and plays** may be underlined or italicized. **Titles of songs, poems, and stories** are set in quotation marks.

<u>Coyotes in the Crosswalk</u> is a book about animals in cities.

Hailey knows most of the words to the song "Catch the Moon."

Use a **colon between the hour and the minute**.

8:36 A.M.          2:20 P.M.          every day at 6:15

Use a **colon before a list of items** if the words before the colon are a complete sentence.

Bring the following items: a sketchbook, paints, and two brushes.

## Putting It Together

Complete each sentence below with a title. Use correct punctuation.

1. My favorite animated movie is _____.

2. I think that _____ would be a great story title.

3. _____ is the funniest book I know.

## Review Dialogue, Titles, and Colons

Read each pair of sentences below. Circle the
letter of the sentence that is written correctly.

1. **a.** The pool is open from 10:0 until 50:0.
   **b.** The pool is open from 1:00 until 5:00.

2. **a.** "It's Raining Pigs and Noodles" is a book of poetry by Jack Prelutsky.
   **b.** *It's Raining Pigs and Noodles* is a book of poetry by Jack Prelutsky.

3. **a.** In the box, there were two books, three CDs, and a photo.
   **b.** In the box, there were: two books, three CDs, and a photo.

4. **a.** The last showing of the movie *Robots* is at 7:40.
   **b.** The last showing of the movie "Robots" is at 7 40.

Proofread the passage below. Add or
delete quotation marks and punctuation
as needed.

| | |
|---|---|
| *e* – deletes punctuation |
| ᵛ – inserts quotations |
| ∧ – inserts punctuation |

Lea and Elizabeth carefully unlatched the trunk Elizabeth found in

attic. "This must have been Mom's dress when she was just a baby, said

Lea, unfolding a tiny blue dress. "I can't believe how tiny she was"!

Elizabeth asked "Did you see all these old books?" She pulled out the

following books and stacked them on the table All-of-a-Kind Family, Little

Women, Anne of Green Gables, and A Child's Garden of Verses.

Lea read the poems Bed in Summer and Land of Counterpane out

loud. We should ask Mom if she read to us from this book when we were

little, said Lea. "I know I've heard these poems before"

NAME_____

When the subject of a sentence is singular, the verb usually ends with **s** or **es**.

Add **s** to most regular verbs that have a single subject.

*Phoebe jumps* rope.      *The tiger races* across the savanna.

Add **es** to regular verbs that have a single subject and end in **o**, **sh**, **ch**, **s**, **x**, and **z**.

*Dad washes* the dinner dishes.
*Corey coaxes* the kitten from her hiding place.

If the verb ends in **y**, drop the **y** and add **ies**.

*We worry* about the storm.    *Will worries* about the storm.

When the subject is plural, the verb does not end with **s** or **es**.

*Akiko and Dustin live* in the same apartment building.
*The puppies play* with the rubber toy.

**Complete It**

Read the paragraph below. Circle the verb from the pair in parentheses that correctly completes each sentence.

Joseph Malarkey (invent, invents) things. He (thinks, think) of amazing and interesting ideas. Then, he (try, tries) to create his inventions. Some of them are great successes, and others are not. Joseph has a twin sister named Josefina. Joseph and Josefina (work, works) on many inventions together. For example, they (invents, invent) amazing new recycling machines. You (places, place) cans inside the machine. It (wash, washes) and (dries, dry) the cans, and then it (crushes, crush) them into incredibly tiny pieces. Joseph (push, pushes) the big green button. The pieces (whirl, whirls) inside the machine. In moments, the machine (produce, produces) a brand-new, shiny toy car!

# Lesson 3.1 Subject-Verb Agreement: Adding **s** and **es**

## Proof It

Read the sentences below. Make sure the subject and the verb, or verbs, agree in each sentence. Correct the mistakes you find using proofreading marks.

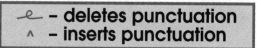
*e* – deletes punctuation
^ – inserts punctuation

1. Every summer, Eduardo and Crista catches tadpoles in Miller Creek.

2. Crista toss the net into the mucky water.

3. Eduardo stand nearby and hold a jar filled with creek water.

4. Eduardo and Crista brings home the tadpoles.

5. Crista supply the tadpoles with food, water, and places to hide.

6. Over time, the tadpoles grows legs and loses their gills and tail.

7. The children watches the curious creatures change into frogs.

8. They carefully carries the young frogs back to Miller Creek.

9. Eduardo and Crista releases the frogs at the edge of the creek and watches as they hops away.

## Try It

1. Write a sentence about something you do every summer. Underline the subject, and circle the verb.

_____

2. Now, use a plural subject and write a sentence about something that people do every winter. Underline the subject, and circle the verb.

_____

## Lesson 3.2  Regular Past-Tense Verbs

**Past-tense verbs** tell about things that have already happened. To change most regular verbs to the past tense, add **ed**. If the verb already ends in **e**, just add **d**.

> Chase *wanted* a green balloon.
> The movers *lifted* the boxes into the truck.
> Melanie *skated* around the pond.

If a verb ends in **y**, change the **y** to **i** and add **ed**.

> The nurses *apply* pressure to the wound.
> The nurses *applied* pressure to the wound.

### Identify It

Read the sentences below. Circle the present-tense verb in each sentence. Then, write the past tense of the verb on the line.

1. _____ Eleanor Roosevelt serves as First Lady from 1933 until 1945.

2. _____ She believes in human rights for all people.

3. _____ She supports the Civil Rights Movement.

4. _____ As a teenager, Eleanor studies at a London boarding school.

5. _____ Eleanor and Franklin Roosevelt marry in 1905.

6. _____ During World War I, Eleanor visits wounded soldiers.

7. _____ Later, she creates programs for children, women, and minorities.

8. _____ In her spare time, Eleanor enjoys traveling and archery.

## Lesson 3.2 Regular Past-Tense Verbs

**Complete It**

Read the sentences below. Complete each sentence with the past tense of the verb in parentheses.

1. New Yorkers _____ Hillary Clinton to the Senate while she was still First Lady. (elect)

2. Abigail Adams's grandson _____ the letters she wrote to her husband, President Adams. (publish)

3. Grace Coolidge _____ as a teacher of hearing-impaired children. (work)

4. Lady Bird Johnson _____ to 33 foreign countries as wife of the vice-president. (travel)

5. Laura Bush _____ library science at the University of Texas. (study)

6. Edith Roosevelt _____ books and reading. (love)

7. As first lady, Rosalynn Carter _____ to bring attention to the performing arts. (try)

8. Lou Hoover _____ camping, hunting, riding horses, and geology. (enjoy)

**Try It**

Write two sentences in the present tense on a separate sheet of paper. Be sure to use regular verbs in your sentences. Rewrite your sentences in the past tense on the lines below.

1. _____

2. _____

## Lesson 3.3  Irregular Past-Tense Verbs: *Fell, Dug, Began, Took, Sang*

The **past tense** of some verbs is irregular. Instead of adding **ed** or **d** to form the past tenses of these verbs, you need to memorize the past-tense forms.

| Present Tense | Past Tense |
|---|---|
| the leaves *fall* | the leaves *fell* |
| the chipmunks *dig* | the chipmunks *dug* |
| the story *begins* | the story *began* |
| we *take* the dog | we *took* the dog |
| Dad *sings* | Dad *sang* |

**Complete It**

Each pair of sentences below is written in the past and the present tense. Fill in the spaces with past- or present-tense verbs to complete the sentences.

1. Present Tense: Everyone _____ the National Anthem.
   Past Tense: Everyone sang the National Anthem.

2. Present Tense: The archaeologists dig for clues.
   Past Tense: The archaeologists _____ for clues.

3. Present Tense: Adam takes some herbs from the garden.
   Past Tense: Adam _____ some herbs from the garden.

4. Present Tense: The day begins with the beeping alarm.
   Past Tense: The day _____ with the beeping alarm.

5. Present Tense: Mrs. Bickleton falls on a patch of ice.
   Past Tense: Mrs. Bickleton _____ on a patch of ice.

6. Present Tense: Lulu _____ a hole for the chestnut tree.
   Past Tense: Lulu dug a hole for the chestnut tree.

7. Present Tense: The movie _____ with a funny scene.
   Past Tense: The movie began with a funny scene.

Irregular Past-Tense Verbs: *Fell, Dug, Began, Took, Sang*

NAME _____

## Solve It

Read each sentence below. Circle the verb. In the space, write the past tense of the verb. Then, find each past-tense verb in the word search puzzle.

1. The mole digs its tunnel far beneath the garden.

   _____

2. The dead tree falls with an enormous crash. _____

3. Mom sings the same lullaby to my baby brother every night.

   _____

4. The concert begins at 8:00.

   _____

5. Annabelle takes violin lessons.

   _____

| g | f | j | d | e | s | w |
|---|---|---|---|---|---|---|
| h | n | f | u | d | a | m |
| o | b | e | g | a | n | k |
| e | d | l | q | i | g | c |
| b | r | l | t | o | o | k |
| s | f | j | a | d | y | p |

## Try It

Write a short paragraph on the lines below. Use the past tense of three of the following verbs in your paragraph: *fall, dig, begin, take,* or *sing.*

_____

_____

_____

_____

_____

_____

# Lesson 3.4 Irregular Past-Tense Verbs: *Spoke, Drew, Broke, Caught, Left*

The **past tense** of some verbs is irregular. Instead of adding **ed** or **d** to form the past tenses of these verbs, you need to memorize the past-tense forms.

| Present Tense | Past Tense |
|---|---|
| we *speak* | we *spoke* |
| Doug *draws* | Doug *drew* |
| the egg *breaks* | the egg *broke* |
| Amelia *catches* | Amelia *caught* |
| we *leave* | we *left* |

**Rewrite It**

The sentences below are all in the present tense. Rewrite them in the past tense.

1. The Howards accidentally leave the back window open.

   _____

2. They catch a confused bat flying around the house.

   _____

3. Mr. Howard breaks a vase sitting on the fireplace mantel.

   _____

4. Lara Howard draws a picture of the bat for her afternoon art class.

   _____

5. Mrs. Howard speaks with the bat expert at the Nature Center.

   _____

# Lesson 3.4 Irregular Past-Tense Verbs: *Spoke, Drew, Broke, Caught, Left*

## Proof It

Read the diary entry below. Find the seven verbs that are in the wrong tense or that are spelled incorrectly. Use proofreading marks to correct the mistakes.

| ℯ – deletes words or letters |
| ^ – inserts words or letters |

Sunday, August 22

Dear Diary,

It has been a crazy week! I catched a cold just a few days before we leaved for the family reunion. Luckily, it lasted for only two days. Dad speaked to Uncle Albert on the phone. He told Dad that more than 40 members of our family would be coming to this reunion!

We catch the train at 8:00 on Friday morning. We almost missed it because two wheels on Mom's suitcase breaked. There wasn't time to fix them, so we had to run for the train carrying the suitcase. Dad speaks to the ticket agent, and he held the train for us. The train leaves the station at 8:06, and we were on our way to the Delregno family reunion in Boston!

## Try It

The verb *catch* can be used in several different ways. On the lines below, write two sentences in the past tense about different things you can catch.

_____

_____

# Review Subject-Verb Agreement and Regular and Irregular Past-Tense Verbs

When the subject of a sentence is singular, the verb usually ends with **s** or **es**. Add **s** to regular verbs that have a singular subject. Add **es** if the verb ends with **o**, **sh**, **ch**, **s**, **x**, or **z**.

*Austin swims* at the community pool.  *Mason pitches* the ball.

If the verb ends in **y**, drop the **y** and add **ies**.

They always *hurry* in the morning.  He always *hurries* in the morning.

When the subject is plural, the verb does not end with **s** or **es**.

*The fans* **cheer** for their favorite players.

To change most regular verbs to the past tense, add **ed**. If the verb already ends in **e**, just add **d**.

The scientist *discovered* a cure.  Matt *raked* the leaves.

If a verb ends in **y**, change the **y** to **i** and add **ed**.

Bailey and Scott *cry* at the movie.  Bailey *cried* at the movie.

The past tenses of some verbs are irregular. Instead of adding **ed** or **d**, you need to memorize the past-tense forms.

| | | |
|---|---|---|
| fall → fell | speak → spoke | dig → dug |
| draw → drew | begin → began | break → broke |
| take → took | catch → caught | sing → sang |
| leave → left | | |

## Putting It Together

Read each sentence below. Then, circle the verb from the pair in parentheses that best completes each sentence.

1. The opossum (waddle, waddles) across the street.

2. The raccoons (look, looks) for food in the trashcan.

3. A bat (flies, fly) across the sky at twilight.

# Review Subject-Verb Agreement and Regular and Irregular Past-Tense Verbs

The verbs in bold are in the present tense. Write the past-tense form of each verb on the line.

1. The moonflower **blooms** in the middle of the night. _____

2. The bushbaby **leaps** from branch to branch in the bright moonlight.
   _____

3. Late at night, the skunk **digs** in the garden in search of insects.
   _____

4. Debbie **plants** an evening primrose next to her bedroom window.
   _____

5. The whippoorwill **catches** insects as they flew through the night air.
   _____

6. I fell asleep as the crickets **sing** in the summer evening. _____

7. Dozens of moths **gather** around the bright porch light. _____

Read the clues below. Write the answers in the numbered spaces in the crossword puzzle.

Across
**2** past tense of *whisper*
**4** past tense of *leave*
**5** present tense of *broke*
**7** past tense of *discover*

Down
**1** past tense of *carry*
**2** past tense of *worry*
**3** past tense of *speak*
**6** present tense of *fried*

REVIEW

## Lesson 3.5 Forming the Future Tense

There are three main verb tenses: the past tense, the present tense, and the future tense. The **past tense** describes things that have already happened. The **present tense** describes things that are happening right now. The **future tense** describes something that will take place in the future.

> **Past:** The members of the band *marched* down Main Street.
> **Present:** The members of the band *march* down Main Street.
> **Future:** The members of the band *will march* down Main Street.

Form the future tense by using the word *will* with a verb.

> The library **will** *close* at 5:00.     The pretzels **will** *bake* for 35 minutes.
>
> Andre **will** *graduate* in June.     Zan **will** *draw* your portrait.

**Identify It**

Read each sentence below. If it is in the future tense, make a check mark on the line. If it is not, write the future tense of the verb on the line.

1. _____ Twenty years from now, life will be very different.

2. _____ Every day, scientists and inventors make new discoveries.

3. _____ Refrigerators of the future will be smart, according to scientists.

4. _____ They tell you what ingredients you need to make a certain dish.

5. _____ These amazing refrigerators will even help you plan a balanced diet!

6. _____ People rely on computers for many things every day.

7. _____ Computers and tiny radio transmitters will create smarter kitchens in the future.

## Lesson 3.5  Forming the Future Tense

**Rewrite It**

In the space before each sentence, write **PA** if the sentence takes place in the past. Write **PR** if it takes place in the present. Then, rewrite each sentence in the future tense.

1. _____ Clothes of the future have many interesting features.

   _____

2. _____ They are made of a special kind of material.

   _____

3. _____ This incredible new material always stays dry and clean.

   _____

4. _____ Another type of material contained tiny electric fibers.

   _____

5. _____ People listened to their clothes like radios.

   _____

6. _____ The clothes even change color and patterns.

   _____

**Try It**

Use your imagination to think of an invention that could make life easier for people of the future. Write a short paragraph in the future tense that describes what your invention will do.

_____

_____

_____

## Lesson 3.6 Tricky Verb Usage

Certain verbs are easily confused with one another. Sometimes, using these words correctly takes a little bit of extra thought.

The verb *lie* can mean *to rest in a flat position*. The past tense of *lie* is *lay*.

      Ryan has a headache, so he is going to *lie* down.

      Ryan *lay* on the bed until he felt better.

*Lay* can also mean *to put or place*. The past tense of *lay* is *laid*.

      Mia *lay* the papers down.        Mia *laid* the papers down.

The verb *sit* means *to be in a seated position*. The past tense of *sit* is *sat*.

      Ethan *sits* on the front stoop.     Ethan *sat* on the front stoop.

*Set* can mean *to put or place*. The past and present tense are the same.

      I *set* the table.            Yesterday, I *set* the table.

*Can* means *able to*. *May* means *allowed to*.

      I *can* juggle six balls. (I *am able to* juggle six balls)

      You *may* stay up until midnight on New Year's Eve. (You *are allowed to* stay up.)

### Complete It

Underline the word in parentheses that correctly completes each sentence.

1. Imani (set, sat) at a table in the Make It and Bake It Pottery Studio.

2. She (lied, laid) out all the paints she planned to use.

3. "(May, Can) I use these paintbrushes?" Imani asked Jenna, the owner.

4. Jenna nodded. "I will (sit, set) them here so you can reach them."

5. "I (may, can) paint flowers, but people are harder, "said Imani.

6. When Imani was done, Jenna (set, sat) the dishes in the kiln to bake.

# Lesson 3.6 Tricky Verb Usage

**Proof It**

Read the sentences below. Use proofreading marks to correct the eight verbs that are used incorrectly.

| | |
|---|---|
| _e_ | – **deletes words or letters** |
| ^ | – **inserts words or letters** |

Imani carried the painted bowl and flowerpot into her room. She carefully sat them on a high shelf in her closet. Suddenly, there was a knock on her door. Imani quickly lied down on her bed and pretended to look at a book.

"Can I come in?" asked Imani's mom, opening the door a crack.

"Sure," said Imani. Her mom lay a stack of neatly folded laundry on the dresser and set down on the bed.

"Do you feel okay?" she asked. "It's not like you to come home and lay down right away."

"I feel fine," replied Imani, setting up. "I was just a little tired this afternoon. I may put away my own laundry," she added quickly, when she saw her mom heading for the closet.

"Phew," said Imani, as her mom went back downstairs a moment later. "I need to find a better hiding place for my pottery. Mom's birthday is still a week away!"

Forming the Future Tense and
Tricky Verb Usage

**Past, present,** and **future** are the three main verb tenses. They are used to refer to things that have already happened, that are happening right now, and that will happen in the future.

Form the **future tense** by using the word *will* with a verb.

The baby-sitter *will* be here soon.

Bethany *will* read your story.

Some words are easily confused with one another. Refer to the examples below if you need help remembering which word to use.

*lie* = to rest in a flat position (past tense is *lay*)

*lay* = to put or place (past tense is *laid*)

*sit* = to be in a seated position (past tense is *sat*)

*set* = to put or place (past tense is *set*)

*can* = able to                    *may* = allowed to

**Putting It Together**

Complete each sentence below with a word from the box.

| lie | lay | laid | sit | sat | set | can | may |
|-----|-----|------|-----|-----|-----|-----|-----|

1. Mr. Damian put down his briefcase and _____ the mail on the table.

2. You _____ have some pudding when you finish your dinner.

3. If you _____ down on the paper, I can trace the outline of your body.

4. Sabrina _____ on the porch step and waited for the rain to stop.

5. George _____ do 25 push-ups.

6. Please _____ the can of paint on the newspapers.

# Review Forming the Future Tense and Tricky Verb Usage

Read the sentences below, and circle the verbs. Write *past*, *present*, or *future* on the line to show the verb tense.

1. The Winter Olympics occur every four years. _____

2. The first Olympic Games were held in 1896 in Athens, Greece.

   _____

3. The Summer Games and the Winter Games are held in different years.

   _____

4. The 2008 Summer Games will be in Beijing, China. _____

5. Vancouver, Canada, will host the 2010 Winter Olympics. _____

6. The Olympic flag shows five linked rings in blue, yellow, black, green, and red. _____

7. The flag was used for the first time in 1920 in Antwerp, Belgium.

   _____

Complete each sentence with the future tense of the verb in parentheses.

1. Who _____ the Olympic Flame at the 2012 Olympics? (light)

2. Thousands of people _____ to China to see the athletes perform. (travel)

3. No one knows which country _____ home the most gold medals. (bring)

4. Do you think the Olympics _____ to your hometown one day? (come)

5. Do you think that sports like golf, bowling, and surfing _____ Olympic sports someday? (be)

## Lesson 3.7  Contractions

A **contraction** is a short way of writing or saying something. When you combine two words in a contraction, an apostrophe (') takes the place of the missing letters.

Often, pronouns and verbs are combined in contractions.

*She is* taking the subway.        *She's* taking the subway.
*They will* ski the difficult slopes.    *They'll* ski the difficult slopes.

Contractions can also be formed with verbs and the word *not*.

Dallas *is not* the capital of Texas.   Dallas *isn't* the capital of Texas.
Lorenzo *does not* like mushrooms.  Lorenzo *doesn't* like mushrooms.

| Tip | In a question, the two words that can form a contraction may not be next to one another. Why *could* you *not* arrive on time? Why *couldn't* you arrive on time? |
|---|---|

**Rewrite It**

Rewrite each sentence below using contractions. The number in parentheses will tell you how many contractions to use.

1. Have Charley and Tess not visited New York City before? (1)

   _____

2. They will go to Times Square and Grand Central Station. (1)

   _____

3. They have planned a spring trip, so it will not be cold outside. (2)

   _____

4. I have asked for a souvenir from the Empire State Building. (1)

   _____

## Lesson 3.7 Contractions

**Proof It**

Read the paragraphs below. Six contractions contain mistakes. Use proofreading marks to correct the mistakes.

> ℯ – **deletes punctuation**
> ˇ – **inserts apostrophe**

Manhattan's Central Park is one of the most famous parks in the world. For New Yorkers, there just isnt any place like it. New York City is covered with buildings and skyscrapers as far as the eye can see. People do'nt have to leave the city to find green space, though. The park rests on 843 acres of land. Human visitors are'nt the only ones to enjoy this green oasis in the city. Birds, bugs, and small mammals make their homes there. Theyr'e easy to spot on a walk through the park.

Many people enjoy the sculptures of Central Park. Frederick Olmsted, one of the park's designers, didn'nt want sculptures in the park. He thought it would look cluttered. Today, the sculptures are a part of the park, and most people cant imagine it without them.

**Try It**

Combine words from the boxes below to form contractions. Write two sentences using the contractions.

| I | he | it | they | can | not | have | is | would |
|---|-----|-----|-------|-------|------|------|-----|-------|
| you | she | we | could | did | will | am | are | |

1. _____

2. _____

NAME _____

# Lesson 3.8 Negative Words and Double Negatives

Words such as *no, none, never, nothing, nobody, nowhere,* and *no one* are **negative words**. The word *not* and contractions with *not* are also negative words. **Double negatives** are sentences with more than one negative word. Do not use double negatives in your writing.

Incorrect
There *isn't nothing* left.

Kris did *not* bring *no* CDs.

Correct
There *isn't* anything left.
There is *nothing* left.

Kris did *not* bring any CDs.
Kris brought *no* CDs.

**Complete It**
Underline the word in parentheses that correctly completes each sentence.

1. I haven't (ever, never) written a letter to the state governor before.

2. I will tell Governor Hernandez that there (isn't, is) nowhere in the state as polluted as Dandelion River.

3. No one can (never, ever) swim or go boating or fishing in the river.

4. There isn't (no, any) reason why companies should be allowed to keep polluting the river.

5. Nobody has ever made the companies do (nothing, anything) to clean up the water.

6. Pollution (has, hasn't) not always been a problem in Dandelion River.

**Tip** The two negatives in a double negative cancel each other out. *I don't want no ice cream* actually means *I do want ice cream.*

NAME _____

## Lesson 3.8 Negative Words and Double Negatives

**Proof It**

There are five double negatives in the letter below. Find each double negative, and correct it using proofreading marks.

> ✏ – deletes words
> ^ – inserts words

April 14

Dear Governor Hernandez,

My name is Alysha Aroya. I am writing to you because I am concerned about Dandelion River. The river was once beautiful. It was a part of my parents' childhoods. Today, no one can't use the river for recreation. Fish and other wildlife cannot live there no longer. People throw litter in the water because they think no one will never do anything to save the river. They believe it is a lost cause.

As long as the big companies in Blue Bend, Florida, don't do nothing to change, the river will stay polluted. They shouldn't never be allowed to do so much damage to the environment.

I am enclosing a list of 100 signatures. The people who signed their names know how important it is to clean up Dandelion River. We hope that you agree and help us make a positive change.

Sincerely,

Alysha Aroya

**Try It**

Write a short paragraph about something in your town or state that you think is worth saving, such as a building or natural area. Correctly use at least three negative words in your writing.

_____

_____

_____

Spectrum Language Arts
Grade 4

Chapter 3 Lesson 8
Usage
113

#  Contractions, Negative Words, and Double Negatives

When you combine two words to form a **contraction**, an apostrophe takes the place of the missing letters.

*I am* in the fifth grade.          *I'm* in the fifth grade.
*He will* forget to bring his lunch.     *He'll* forget to bring his lunch.
Pandas *are not* really bears.      Pandas *aren't* really bears.

*No, none, never, nothing, nobody, nowhere, no one,* and contractions with *not* are **negative words**. Never use a **double negative**, or two negatives together.

**Incorrect:** There *weren't no* free samples left.
**Correct:** There *weren't* any free samples left.
**Correct:** There *were no* free samples left.

## Putting It Together

On the line, write a contraction for each pair of underlined words.

1. _____ Mark Twain <u>was not</u> the real name of the famous Missouri author.

2. _____ Even if you <u>have not</u> read Twain's books, you might have heard of Tom Sawyer.

3. _____ <u>You will</u> probably enjoy reading all about Tom's many adventures.

4. _____ The Adventures of Tom Sawyer <u>is not</u> Twain's only famous book.

5. _____ Twain <u>did not</u> write only fiction stories.

6. _____ He <u>would have</u> loved to spend all his days on the Mississippi River.

7. _____ It might be hard to find a riverboat pilot who <u>does not</u> know all about fellow pilot Mark Twain.

# Review Contractions, Negative Words, and Double Negatives

Circle the word in parentheses that correctly completes each sentence.

1. The Mississippi River (is, isn't) not the longest river in the United States.

2. Historians believe there were not (any, no) Europeans who reached the river before Hernando de Soto in 1541.

3. There was not (nothing, anything) as exciting as the steamboat races on the river in the mid-1800s.

4. If you travel to New Orleans, Memphis, or St. Louis, you (will, won't) not be far from the mighty Mississippi.

5. No one had (never, ever) swum the entire length of the river before Martin Strel in 2002.

Read the paragraph below. Seven contractions contain mistakes. Use proofreading marks to correct the mistakes.

| *e* – deletes punctuation |
| ˅ – inserts apostrophe |

My uncle, Beau, wants to travel down the Mississippi River by raft, just like Mark Twain's Huck Finn. Hes planning the trip with several of his friends. Theyr'e going to make the raft themselves. I think its' amazing that they found instructions for building a raft on the Internet. Captain Benjamin Lee Adams will pilot the raft. Hes' been a riverboat pilot for more than 30 years. My parents were a little worried that Uncle Beau did'nt know what he was getting into. Theyr're relieved that someone with so much experience will be going on the adventure. Uncle Beau says this will be the experience of a lifetime. I hope he is'nt disappointed!

## Lesson 3.9 Regular Plurals

*Singular* means *one*. *Plural* means *more than one*. To change a regular noun from singular to plural, add **s**.

| | | | |
|---|---|---|---|
| Singular: | workbook | dinosaur | tractor |
| Plural: | workbook**s** | dinosaur**s** | tractor**s** |

If a noun ends in **sh**, **ch**, **s**, or **x**, form the plural by adding **es**.

| | | | | |
|---|---|---|---|---|
| Singular: | bea**ch** | fla**sh** | bo**ss** | ta**x** |
| Plural: | beach**es** | flash**es** | boss**es** | tax**es** |

If a noun ends with a consonant and a **y**, form the plural by dropping the **y** and adding **ies**.

| | | | | | |
|---|---|---|---|---|---|
| Singular: | cherr**y** | bab**y** | diar**y** | lad**y** | penn**y** |
| Plural: | cherr**ies** | bab**ies** | diar**ies** | lad**ies** | penn**ies** |

For most nouns that end in **f** or **fe**, form the plural by changing the **f** or **fe** to **ve** and adding **s**.

| | | | | | |
|---|---|---|---|---|---|
| Singular: | shel**f** | lea**f** | kni**fe** | hoo**f** | wi**fe** |
| Plural: | shel**ves** | lea**ves** | kni**ves** | hoo**ves** | wi**ves** |

## Match It

Match each singular word to its plural form. Write the letter of your answer on the line.

1. _____ enemy     **a.** enemies     **b.** enemys

2. _____ wish     **a.** wishs     **b.** wishes

3. _____ sunflower     **a.** sunfloweres     **b.** sunflowers

4. _____ duty     **a.** duteys     **b.** duties

5. _____ wolf     **a.** wolves     **b.** wolfs

6. _____ helicopter     **a.** helicopteres     **b.** helicopters

7. _____ loaf     **a.** loaves     **b.** loafs

# Lesson 3.9  Regular Plurals

## Proof It

Read the paragraphs below. Nine plural words are spelled incorrectly. Use proofreading marks to correct them.

> *e* – deletes words or letters
> ^ – inserts words or letters

The Chinese New Year occurs sometime between January 21 and February 19. The exact date depends on the cycles of the moon. The partys and celebrations last for about two weekes.

Cities and towns are decorated with flowers and paper lanternes in bright colors. People eat special holiday foods. For example, seafood, dumplings, noodles, and pastrys with seeds are common New Year's dishs. Married couples often give small red packets, or pouchs, as gifts to friends and relatives. These packets usually contain money and are meant to be a sign of good fortune in the coming year.

Dragon dances are a part of the celebrationes. As many as 50 people might wear a single costume. Fireworkses, dragon dances, and other New Year's traditiones can be found in Chinatowns across the United States.

## Try It

Write a short paragraph describing a holiday that you and your family celebrate. Use at least four plural words.

_____

_____

_____

# Lesson 3.10  Irregular Plurals

Some plural words are irregular and do not follow the rules. For example, to form the plural of words that end in **o**, you add **s** or **es**. You must memorize the forms of irregular plurals.

| Singular: | kangaroo | piano | studio | solo | auto |
|---|---|---|---|---|---|
| Plural: | kangaroo**s** | piano**s** | studio**s** | solo**s** | auto**s** |

| Singular: | tomato | echo | hero | potato |
|---|---|---|---|---|
| Plural: | tomato**es** | echo**es** | hero**es** | potato**es** |

For some words, the plural form is totally different than the singular form.

| man → men | foot → feet | louse → lice | ox → oxen |
|---|---|---|---|
| goose → geese | mouse → mice | tooth → teeth | die → dice |
| child → children | woman → women | | |

The singular and plural forms of the following words are the same: *deer, fish, moose, sheep, trout, salmon, cod, series, species, traffic, wheat,* and *offspring.*

## Identify It

Choose the correct version of each sentence below and circle it.

1. **a.** Buy one pound of tomatos.
   **b.** Buy one pound of tomatoes.

2. **a.** How many species of toads are there?
   **b.** How many specieses of toads are there?

3. **a.** Six oxen pulled the cart.
   **b.** Six oxes pulled the cart.

4. **a.** The box can hold photoes or videoes.
   **b.** The box can hold photos or videos.

5. **a.** Which of these radios sounds best?
   **b.** Which of these radioes sounds best?

## Lesson 3.10  Irregular Plurals

**Solve It**

Complete each sentence below with the plural form of the word in parentheses. Use a dictionary if you need help. Then, search for each plural word in the puzzle.

| s | d | f | h | p | n | a | t | r | o |
|---|---|---|---|---|---|---|---|---|---|
| f | g | v | w | q | t | a | o | o | n |
| r | h | c | h | i | l | d | r | e | n |
| b | a | k | e | z | j | l | p | i | p |
| w | p | i | a | n | o | s | e | f | n |
| v | e | u | t | d | s | f | d | b | o |
| r | t | n | a | p | t | r | o | u | t |
| q | l | x | u | f | a | y | e | j | n |
| p | o | t | a | t | o | e | s | f | k |

1. The movers carefully carried two _____ up a steep flight of stairs. (piano)

2. How many _____ will be at the picnic? (child)

3. Michi and her dad caught three rainbow _____ when they went to the lake. (trout)

4. The tour guide showed us several _____ that were used in World War II. (torpedo)

5. The field of _____ looked golden in the sun. (wheat)

6. We grew _____, zucchini, and peppers. (potato)

**Try It**

Write two sentences using the plural forms of at least two of the following words: *man, hero, woman, deer, auto, photo, potato, mouse, sheep, zoo.*

_____

_____

## Lesson 3.11 Singular Possessives

To form the **possessive** of a singular noun, add an apostrophe (') and the letter **s** to the end of the word. This indicates that the person or thing is the owner of the object that follows the possessive.

the boat**'s** deck the telescope**'s** lens Malik**'s** vacation
Nissa**'s** party the pig**'s** trough Ms. Nilsson**'s** flowers

**Complete It**

Write the possessive form of each noun in parentheses to complete the sentences below.

1. _____ job is to study chimpanzees in the wild. (Jane Goodall)

2. This _____ work has broken new ground in the study of animals and science. (zoologist)

3. _____ discovery that chimpanzees make and use tools was very important. (Jane)

4. The _____ behavior often amuses and surprises Jane. (chimp)

5. Jane has watched _____ nine children grow up. (Fifi)

6. Jane and her husband studied other African animals on _____ Serengeti Plain. (Tanzania)

7. Her _____ work has been to preserve wild animals and places. (life)

# Lesson 3.11 Singular Possessives

**Rewrite It**

Rewrite each sentence below. Replace the words in parentheses with a possessive.

1. (The books of the scientist) describe her experiences at Gombe National Park.

   _____

   _____

2. Jane gives much credit to (the encouragement of her mother).

   _____

   _____

3. (The face of a chimp) can show emotions like joy, fear, sadness, surprise, and amusement.

   _____

   _____

4. (The rain forests of Africa) make a good home for chimps, but they are quickly disappearing.

   _____

   _____

**Try It**

Write a sentence about a person who has an interesting career. Use a possessive in your sentence.

   _____

   _____

## Lesson 3.12 Plural Possessives

To form the **possessive of a plural word** that ends in **s**, add an apostrophe after the **s**.

the flags' colors                    the athletes' equipment
the computers' screens          the cars' engines
the students' homework         the birds' feathers

For plural words that do not end in **s**, add an apostrophe and an **s** to form the possessive.

the teeth**'s** size      the people**'s** ideas          the women**'s** clothing

Do not mistake a plural for a possessive. Possessives always have an apostrophe.

<u>Plural:</u>        trees          zebras          the Johnsons
<u>Possessive:</u> trees' leaves   zebras' stripes   the Johnsons' apartment

**Identify It**

Read each phrase below. If it is plural, write **PL** in the space. If it is singular possessive, write **SP**. If it is plural possessive, write **PP**.

1. _____ the basketball players' jerseys

2. _____ both of the referees

3. _____ the home team's advantage

4. _____ the fans' cheers

5. _____ the stadium's location

6. _____ the teams' coaches

7. _____ the members of the team

8. _____ the Minnesota Timberwolves

## Lesson 3.12  Plural Possessives

### Proof It

Read the diary entry below. There are six plural possessives that are missing apostrophes or have apostrophes in the wrong places. Use proofreading marks to correct the errors.

| |
|---|
| ℓ – **deletes punctuation** |
| ˅ – **inserts apostrophe** |

October 18

Dear Diary,

Yesterday, I went to my first professional basketball game. The fans screams were incredibly loud as the players jogged onto the court. The announcers voices kept us informed of every play. At halftime, Dad and I went exploring. We brought our programs with us. I was hoping to run into some of the players and get autographs. No luck, though!

The last quarter of the game was very intense. Both team's coaches looked worried. The Lakers were up by only two points, and I knew it was still anyone's game. There were large screens mounted all around the stadium. We could see the expressions on all the player's faces and every move they made.

With only three seconds remaining, the Lakers forward made a free throw. I held my breath as the ball smoothly sailed through the net. The buzzers sound signaled the end of the game. I can't wait to go to another pro game!

# Review  Regular and Irregular Plurals and Singular and Plural Possessives

To form the **plural** of regular, singular nouns, add **s**.

balloon ➔ balloon**s**    flower ➔ flower**s**    snack ➔ snack**s**

If a noun ends in **sh**, **ch**, **s**, or **x**, form the plural by adding **es**.

bran**ch** ➔ bran**ches**    a**x** ➔ ax**es**    cla**ss** ➔ class**es**

If a noun ends with a consonant and a **y**, drop the **y** and add **ies**.

countr**y** ➔ countr**ies**    pon**y** ➔ pon**ies**    dut**y** ➔ dut**ies**

If a noun ends in **f** or **fe**, change the **f** or **fe** to **ve** and add **s**.

hoo**f** ➔ hoo**ves**    sel**f** ➔ sel**ves**    kni**fe** ➔ kni**ves**

**Irregular plurals** do not follow these rules. The plural form may be completely different, or the singular and plural forms may be the same.

tooth ➔ teeth    ox ➔ oxen    moose ➔ moose

To form the plural of words that end in **o**, sometimes you add **s**, and other times you add **es**. Memorize the plural forms, and use a dictionary if you need to.

auto ➔ auto**s**    studio ➔ studio**s**    hero ➔ hero**es**

Add an apostrophe and an **s** to the end of a singular noun to form the **possessive**. To form the **plural possessive** of a word that ends in **s**, just add an apostrophe after the **s**.

Singular Possessive:    Hardy**'s** laughter    the book**'s** cover
the camera**'s** photos

Plural Possessive:    the boys**'** laughter    the books**'** covers
the cameras**'** photos

# Review Regular and Irregular Plurals and Singular and Plural Possessives

## Putting It Together

Complete the chart below using the correct form of each noun.

| Singular | Plural | Plural Possessive | |
|---|---|---|---|
| zoo | _____ | _____ | animals |
| _____ | loaves | _____ | crusts |
| sheep | _____ | sheep's wool | |
| fairy | _____ | _____ | wings |
| artist | _____ | artists' paintings | |
| _____ | _____ | bushes' branches | |
| clock | clocks | _____ | hands |

Read the sentences below. There are nine mistakes with plurals. There are four mistakes with possessives. Use proofreading marks to correct the errors.

| | |
|---|---|
| ℓ | – deletes letters and punctuation |
| ∧ | – inserts letters and punctuation |
| ⌄ | – inserts apostrophes |

1. There are two pianoes in the music room at Ross' school.

2. Three of the sopranoes in the girls's choir have soloes.

3. The choir directors sister gives trumpet lessons twice a week.

4. You can find the sheet music on the shelfs in the closet.

5. There are so many varietys of instrumentes that Hitomi can't decide which to try next.

6. Each of the Blankenships's four childs plays a different instrument.

7. After the performance, familys can have some pastrys and punch.

## Lesson 3.13  Subject and Object Pronouns

A **subject pronoun** can be the subject of a sentence, or it can be part of a compound subject. *I, you, he, she, it, we,* and *they* are subject pronouns.

>*Eagles, hawks, owls, and vultures* are raptors.   *They* are raptors.
>*The Adventure Science Center* is in Nashville.   *It* is in Nashville.

When talking about yourself and someone else, always put the other person before you.

>*Grandpa and I* like to do crossword puzzles.
>*He and I* have a lot in common.

**Object pronouns** often follow action verbs or prepositions like *to, at, from, with,* and *of.* Some object pronouns are *me, you, him, her, it, us,* and *them.*

>Please give the DVDs to *Diego.*   Please give the DVDs *to **him**.*
>Gordon won *the race*!   Gordon *won **it**!*

If you use the pronoun *me* or *us* as part of a compound object, *me* or *us* comes after the other part of the compound.

>The day was exciting for our *parents and **us**.*

### Identify It

Read the sentences below. The letters in parentheses will tell you to underline the subject pronoun (**SP**) or the object pronoun (**OP**).

1. My family and I went to the Foods of All Nations Festival. (SP)

2. We sampled foods from 13 countries. (SP)

3. Louis and Mom liked the Indian food best. They are going to make naan at home. (SP)

4. Dad loves Greek food. He has baked baklava for us many times. (OP)

5. Guacamole is a Mexican avocado dip. We ate it with fresh salsa and tortilla chips. (OP)

6. Jalapeño peppers are too spicy for Dad and me. (OP)

## Lesson 3.13  Subject and Object Pronouns

**Proof It**

Read the paragraphs below. Eight pronouns are used incorrectly. They
may also be in the wrong places in the sentence.
Use proofreading marks to correct the mistakes.

| | |
|---|---|
| _e_ | – **deletes words** |
| ^ | – **inserts words** |

Dad ordered some hummus at a Middle Eastern booth. It is made from
ground chickpeas, and me and Louis weren't sure we'd like it. Dad gave
us and Mom some hummus with pita bread. It was delicious.

Louis got some fried plantains and conch fritters at a Jamaican booth.
Mom asked he what they tasted like. Him told her that the plantains tasted
like bananas. He couldn't describe the conch fritters, so us each tried one.

Finally, it was time for dessert. Everyone in my family was feeling full, so
us decided to order two dishes and share them. Trifle is an English dessert. It
is made of sponge cake, custard, and fresh fruit. Dad also ordered some
Japanese green-tea ice cream. Me and Mom loved it, but Louis thought it
wasn't sweet enough. Tasting different foods at the festival made I think
that I might like to be a chef someday.

**Try It**

On the lines below, write a short paragraph about some interesting foods
you have tried or would like to try. Use one object pronoun and two
subject pronouns in your paragraph. Underline the pronouns.

_____

_____

_____

NAME _____

## Lesson 3.14  Comparative Adjectives

Add **er** or **est** to an adjective to make a comparison.

> The giraffe is *taller* than the elephant.
> It is the *tallest* land mammal on Earth.

For adjectives that end in **e**, just add **r** or **st**. For adjectives that end in a consonant and a **y**, drop the **y** and add **ier** or **iest**.

> wis**e**, wis**er**, wis**est**   fluff**y**, fluff**ier**, fluff**iest**   lonel**y**, lonel**ier**, lonel**iest**

For some adjectives, double the final consonant before adding the ending.

> big, bi**gger**, bi**ggest**   thin, thi**nner**, thi**nnest**   dim, di**mmer**, di**mmest**

For adjectives that have two or more syllables, use more or most instead of adding an ending.

> She was the *most helpful* tour guide.
> Kim was *more excited* than Jamal.

Some comparative adjectives change completely with each form.

> good, better, best   bad, worse, worst

**Complete It**

Read each sentence below. Complete it with the correct comparative form of the adjective in parentheses.

1. On average, it is _____ on New Hampshire's Mount Washington than it is in Buffalo, New York. (windy)

2. The _____ flying bird is the peregrine falcon. (fast)

3. Saffron is the _____ spice in the world. (expensive)

4. The world's _____ spider is the 11-inch long Goliath birdeater. (large)

5. It is usually _____ in the Northwest than the Southwest. (wet)

Spectrum Language Arts
Grade 4
128

Chapter 3 Lesson 14
Usage

## Lesson 3.14  Comparative Adjectives

**Proof It**

Read the paragraphs below. Find and correct the nine incorrect comparative adjectives.

| ℓ - deletes words |
| ^ - inserts words |

The students in Edward's class were trying to find a way to set a Guinness World Record. They decided that it wasn't a good idea to try to perform the dangerousest stunts. Anthony joked that he had the smellier feet in the class. Simone said that she could eat spicyer food than anyone she knew. Shankar and Katrina had a contest to see who could blow a biger bubble with chewing gum. Their bubbles weren't even close in size to the bigest bubble ever blown.

"This is hard," said Edward, after hours of brainstorming. "We're not louder or faster or funnyer or amazinger than any other kids," he said.

"I have an idea," said Katrina. "Could we be the generousest class? We could hold lots of fundraisers. We could volunteer for charity events. We could hold clothes drives and food drives."

"That's a great idea, Katrina," said Shankar. "I don't know if it's been done, but we can try to be the world's kinder class!"

**Try It**

Invent three new categories for world's records. Each category should include a comparative adjective. Write them on the lines below.

_____

_____

## Lesson 3.15 Comparative Adverbs

Like adjectives, adverbs can be used to make **comparisons**. Some adverbs follow the same rules that adjectives do. Add **er** or **est** to these adverbs to make a comparison.

> The youngest boy worked *harder* than the other members of his team.
>
> Darren jumped *highest*, but Kelley swam *faster*.

To make a comparison using adverbs that end in **ly**, add the words *more* or *most*.

> Karim waited **more** *patiently* than his sister.
>
> The stars seemed to shine **most** *brightly* when we were out in the country.

### Identify It

Read each pair of sentences below. Circle the letter of the sentence in which the comparative adverb is used correctly.

1. **a.** Jamie recited his poem more calmly than the other contestants.
   **b.** Jamie recited his poem calmlier than the other contestants.

2. **a.** Nadia whispered most quietly than Kendall and Leo.
   **b.** Nadia whispered more quietly than Kendall and Leo.

3. **a.** The Randalls cheered more joyfully of all the families.
   **b.** The Randalls cheered most joyfully of all the families.

4. **a.** The fifth graders tried harder, but the fourth graders were faster.
   **b.** The fifth graders tried more hard, but the fourth graders were faster.

5. **a.** Maggie walked on the balance beam carefullier than the first two girls.
   **b.** Maggie walked on the balance beam more carefully than the first two girls.

# Lesson 3.15 Comparative Adverbs

**Complete It**

Complete each sentence below with the correct comparative form of the adverb in parentheses.

1. Carly answers the phone _____ than her brother. (cheerfully)

2. Out of all the fish in the sea, the sea horse swims the _____. (slow)

3. Christopher listened to my long story _____ than anyone else did. (patiently)

4. The Pandyas arrived _____ than the Parkers or the Yamamotos. (soon)

5. Aunt Charlotte cooks _____ of all her siblings. (skillfully)

6. The smallest puppy ate _____ than the other puppies from the same litter. (quickly)

7. My dad drives _____ of any member of our family. (fast)

8. At the end of the long hike, Michelle raced to the lake _____ than the other campers. (eagerly)

**Try It**

1. Write a sentence comparing two or more people or things. Use a form of the adverb *proudly*.

   _____

2. Write a sentence comparing two or more people or things. Use a form of the adverb *happily*.

   _____

# Review Subject and Object Pronouns and Comparative Adjectives and Adverbs

**Subject pronouns** are pronouns that can be used as the subject of a sentence. *I, you, he, she, it, we,* and *they* are subject pronouns.

> *We* made fruit salad for the potluck dinner.   *He* is a tennis player.

**Object pronouns** often follow action verbs or prepositions. *Me, you, him, her, it, us,* and *them* are object pronouns.

> Val *called* **them** yesterday.       The postcard is *from* **him**.

When talking about yourself (using the pronouns *I, me,* or *us*) and someone else, always put the other person before you.

> *Taylor and I* are taking an art class.

To make a **comparison** using an adjective, do one of the following:
- add **er** or **est** (sweet, sweet**er**, sweet**est**)
- drop the **y** and add **ier** or **iest** (busy, bus**ier**, bus**iest**)
- double the final consonant before adding the ending (hot, hot<u>t</u>**er**, hot<u>t</u>**est**)
- use *more* or *most* instead of adding an ending (**more** interesting)

To make a **comparison** using an adverb, do one of the following:
- add **er** or **est** to most short adverbs (yelled loud**er**, jumped high**est**)
- use *more* or *most* with adverbs ending in **ly** (**more** safely)

## Putting It Together

Read the sentences below. Circle each pronoun. Write **SP** on the line if it is a subject pronoun. Write **OP** on the line if it is an object pronoun.

1. _____ Shalini and I posted signs for the dog wash.

2. _____ We placed the signs on bulletin boards all over town.

3. _____ Shalini's brothers helped us set everything up.

4. _____ Shalini thanked them for helping.

NAME _____

Read the paragraphs below. They contain five mistakes with pronouns and seven mistakes with comparative adjectives and adverbs. Use proofreading marks to correct the mistakes.

It was sunnyer on the day of the dog wash than it had been all week.

> ℓ – deletes words or letters
> ∧ – inserts words or letters

Shalini and me had brought our hoses, shampoo, buckets, and towels to the park. We were ready to start washing, but no one came. Shalini waited more patient than I did, but both of we were anxious. Suddenly, three people arrived with their dogs, and me and Shalini were in business!

As the day went on, we became weter and dirtyer. The bigest dog we washed was a St. Bernard. Him was also the friendlyest dog. He behaved most playfully than the other dogs when us sprayed him with water. By the end of the day, we were tired but proud. We had earned 60 dollars!

Fill in the spaces in the chart with the correct comparative form of the adjectives and adverbs.

| tiny | _____ | tiniest |
| _____ | worse | _____ |
| happily | more happily | _____ |
| clean | _____ | cleanest |
| thin | _____ | _____ |
| _____ | more carefully | _____ |
| _____ | _____ | fluffiest |

# Lesson 3.16   Synonyms and Antonyms

**Synonyms** are words that have the same, or almost the same, meaning. Using synonyms can help you avoid repeating words and can make your writing more interesting.

| | | |
|---|---|---|
| close, near | choose, select | break, shatter |
| yell, scream | sad, unhappy | grin, smile |

**Antonyms** are words that have opposite meanings.

| | | |
|---|---|---|
| true, false | exciting, boring | rough, gentle |
| dark, light | shout, whisper | quickly, slowly |

## Identify It

Read each sentence below. If the word in parentheses is a synonym for the underlined word, write **S** on the line. If it is an antonym, write **A**.

1. Anyone who <u>likes</u> caves should visit Mammoth Cave in Kentucky. (enjoys) _____

2. Mammoth Cave is the <u>largest</u> cave system in the world. (smallest) _____

3. The caves <u>stretch</u> for more than 350 miles. (extend) _____

4. Echo River is on the <u>lowest</u> of the five levels. (highest) _____

5. <u>Rare</u> types of crayfish and blind fish live in the river. (common) _____

6. The caves are <u>always</u> about 54 degrees. (never) _____

7. Mammoth Cave is one of the world's <u>amazing</u> natural wonders. (incredible) _____

> **Tip**   A **thesaurus** is a type of dictionary. Instead of containing definitions, it lists synonyms. A thesaurus can be a helpful tool for writers.

## Lesson 3.16 Synonyms and Antonyms

**Solve It**

Read the clues below. Choose the answers from the box, and write them in the numbered spaces in the crossword puzzle.

| difficult | below | different | narrow | strong |
|---|---|---|---|---|
| mistake | real | bravery | open | easy |

### Across

1 antonym of *same*
4 synonym of *courage*
6 synonym of *error*
8 antonym of *closed*
9 synonym of *under*

### Down

1 antonym of *easy*
2 antonym of *wide*
3 antonym of *weak*
5 antonym of *fake*
7 synonym of *simple*

**Try It**

1. Write a sentence using two of the following words: *giggle, grin, huge, wonderful, finish, break.*

_____

2. Now, rewrite your sentence using synonyms for the two words you chose.

_____

Spectrum Language Arts
Grade 4

Chapter 3 Lesson 16
Usage
**135**

## Lesson 3.17  Homophones

**Homophones** are words that sound alike but have different spellings and meanings. Use the context of a sentence to decide which homophone to use.

We leave in *eight* hours.                  Timmy *ate* the rest of the cereal.
*Their* dog keeps barking.                  *There* is the key!
The opossum's *tail* is hairless.           I have heard you tell this *tale*.
Jackson *threw* the football.               The termites chewed *through* it.

### Complete It

Read each sentence below. Circle the homophone from the pair in parentheses that correctly completes the sentence.

1. Praying mantises have sharp hooks on (their, they're) legs.

2. If you walk around the garden with (bear, bare) feet, you might get stung by a bee.

3. The hummingbird sipped nectar from the brightly-colored (flour, flower).

4. We planted two small (pear, pair) trees in the backyard.

5. If the (weather, whether) is nice tomorrow, we can plant the seedlings.

6. I already (new, knew) how to tell a ladybug from a cucumber beetle.

> **Tip**
>
> If you have trouble remembering which homophone is which, try making up a way to help yourself keep the meanings and spellings straight. For example, some people confuse the homophones *principal* and *principle*. To help yourself remember which is which, think of the school's princi**pal** as your *pal*.

## Lesson 3.17  Homophones

### Proof It

Read the flyer below. Thirteen homophones are used incorrectly. Use proofreading marks to correct the mistakes.

> *e* – deletes words or letters
> ^ – inserts words or letters

---

# WINDING CREAK GARDENING CENTER

### 1736 WELLSPRING RODE

### (842) 555-6824

LEARN HOW TO BILLED YOUR OWN BIRDHOUSE AT 2:00 ON SATURDAY, JUNE 20.

SUMMER SAIL—SAVE 20% TO 50% ON PLANTS AND GARDEN TOOLS. YOU'LL FINED PLENTY OF BARGAINS.

WHY NOT PLANT SOME FLOWERING TREES AND BUSHES?

YOU'LL ENJOY THE SENT ALL SUMMER LONG!

CHECK OUT HOUR HERB AND VEGETABLE SEEDLINGS.

WE ALSO CARRY ALL KINDS OF GARDENING CLOSE,

INCLUDING HATS, SHOES, GLOVES, AND PANTS.

TAKE A MOMENT TO PEAK IN OUR GREENHOUSE

WEAR WE GROW RARE AND EXOTIC PLANTS.

THERE IS NO KNEAD TO HURRY—TAKE YOU'RE THYME

AND ENJOY THE PLANTS.

---

### Try It

On the lines below, write your own advertisement or flyer for a company you've invented. In your ad, use homophones for at least three of the following words: *ate, hour, won, reel, write, hole, hear, cell, wear, you're, sum, wood.*

_____

_____

_____

NAME _____

## Lesson 3.18  Multiple-Meaning Words

**Multiple-meaning words**, also called **homographs**, are words that are spelled the same but have different meanings.

For example, *second* can mean *number two*, or it can mean *a moment in time*.

> The *second* book in the series is the best.
> I'll be finished in just a *second*.

The word *cold* can mean *an illness*, or it can mean *at a low temperature*.

> Parker caught a *cold* from Sydney.
> Use an ice pack to keep the food *cold*.

**Find It**

The following dictionary entry shows two different meanings for the same word. Use it to answer the questions below.

> **bark** *noun* the outer layer of a tree
>    *verb* the sound a dog makes

1. The *bark* of a birch tree is white and peels easily.
   Which definition of bark is used in this sentence? _____
   **a.** the first definition          **b.** the second definition

2. The dog *barked* when he heard his owner's car in the driveway.
   Which definition of bark is used in this sentence? _____
   **a.** the first definition          **b.** the second definition

3. What part of speech is *bark* when it is used to mean *the outer layer of a tree*? _____
   **a.** a noun          **b.** a verb

4. Use the verb *bark* in a sentence.

   _____

   _____

Spectrum Language Arts
Grade 4
138

Chapter 3 Lesson 18
Usage

## Lesson 3.18  Multiple-Meaning Words

**Rewrite It**

Read each sentence below. Then, write a new
sentence using a different meaning for the
underlined word. Use a dictionary if you need help.

1. Tickets to the <u>fair</u> cost four dollars each.

_____

2. I will meet you at the baseball <u>diamond</u> at 4:00.

_____

3. The cast members of the <u>play</u> were excited about opening night.

_____

4. <u>Coat</u> the inside of the pan with cooking spray.

_____

5. Mr. Armand works on the third <u>story</u> of the red brick building.

_____

6. The small frog hid in the weeds that grew along the <u>bank</u> of the river.

_____

**Try It**

1. Write a sentence using a multiple-meaning word. Use *bat, train,
   patient, watch, leaves,* or another multiple-meaning word you know.

_____

2. Now, write a sentence using the other meaning of the word you chose.

_____

# Review Synonyms, Antonyms, Homophones, and Multiple-Meaning Words

**Synonyms** are words that have the same, or almost the same, meaning.

    answer, response      finish, complete      insect, bug

**Antonyms** are words that have opposite meanings.

    wide, narrow      never, always      capture, release

**Homophones** are words that sound alike but have different spellings and meanings.

    If it *rains*, we won't go.      Jen took the horse's *reins*.

**Multiple-meaning words**, also called **homographs**, are words that are spelled the same but have different meanings.

    The *leaves* are changing.      Enrique *leaves* in the morning.

## Putting It Together

Read each sentence below. Then, choose the sentence in which the underlined word is used the same way as it is in the first sentence. Write the letter of your answer on the line.

1. _____ Did you receive the electric <u>bill</u> yet?
   **a.** The bill comes to $8.56.
   **b.** The duck has a longer bill than the sparrow.

2. _____ My back hurts when I <u>lean</u> to the side.
   **a.** The runner was fit and lean.
   **b.** Lean the umbrella against the wall.

3. _____ Laura's muscles are <u>firm</u> from the exercises she has been doing.
   **a.** There are six members of the law firm.
   **b.** The new mattress is nice and firm.

4. _____ All the letters and papers are stored in a <u>trunk</u> in the attic.
   **a.** Belle found the costumes inside the trunk.
   **b.** The elephant uses its trunk in many ways.

# Review Synonyms, Antonyms, Homophones, and Multiple-Meaning Words

Read each sentence below. If the word in bold print is used correctly, make a check mark on the line. If it is not used correctly, write its homophone on the line.

1. _____ It is hard to **sea** through all the fog.

2. _____ Sheila knew it was noon because the **sun** was directly overhead.

3. _____ Duncan hung the **pale** on a peg in the barn.

4. _____ A row of **beech** trees led up to the house.

5. _____ The **hole** family will attend the neighborhood party.

6. _____ The wind **blue** hard and rattled the windows.

7. _____ If you **brake** the wood into small pieces, we can use it to start the fire.

Read each sentence below. If the underlined words are synonyms, write **S** on the line. If they are antonyms, write **A** on the line.

1. _____ Dillon thought the puzzle would be <u>difficult</u>, but it was actually quite <u>easy</u>.

2. _____ <u>Choose</u> the color you like best, and then let your brother <u>select</u> his favorite.

3. _____ Would you rather we went <u>alone</u> or <u>together</u>?

4. _____ Salim thought the painting looked <u>straight</u>, but as he stepped away, he could see that it was <u>crooked</u>.

5. _____ The <u>amazing</u> athlete has performed many <u>incredible</u> feats.

6. _____ If you place a <u>liquid</u> in the freezer, it will become a <u>solid</u> in just a few hours.

## Lesson 3.19  Similes

A **simile** is a figure of speech that compares two unlike things using the words *like* or *as*. Using similes in your stories or poems can make your writing stronger and more interesting to read. They allow the reader to form a vivid picture of what you are describing.

> Craig sanded the jagged edges until they were smooth.
> Craig sanded *the jagged edges* until they were **as smooth as marble**.

> The lawnmower growled as Celia pushed it across the lawn.
> *The lawnmower growled* **like a hungry bear** as Celia pushed it across the lawn.

**Identify It**

Read the paragraphs below. Find and underline the five similes.

Sumiko and Nori opened the door. The fresh snow sparkled like chips of diamond scattered across the front yard. Sumiko breathed in the fresh, icy air. When she exhaled, she could see the cloud of breath hanging in the air like a small balloon. Nori pulled on his scratchy wool mittens and joined Sumiko on the front step.

"This is amazing," said Nori, shaking his head as he looked around him. Icicles hung like jewels from the trees. There wasn't a single footprint or car track as far as he could see. The outdoors was as quiet as a tomb, except for the occasional crack as the sun melted an icicle and it dropped to the ground.

"Let's go for a walk," suggested Sumiko, as she put on her red knit hat. Sumiko and Nori set off down the quiet street, the snow crunching like popcorn beneath their feet.

NAME _____

## Lesson 3.19  Similes

**Complete It**

Complete each sentence below with a simile.

 1. The field of wildflowers was as colorful _____.

 2. The balloon drifted gently through the air, like _____.

 3. The tapping of rain on the tin roof was as comforting
 _____.

 4. Heath's stomach grumbled noisily, like _____.

 5. As Sara and Brett fearfully opened the door, their hearts beat like
 _____.

 6. The rough, grainy sand felt like _____ on Ilana's
 bare feet.

 7. The tart lemonade tasted as refreshing _____.

 8. As he climbed the steps to the stage, Jacob was as nervous
 _____.

**Try It**

Imagine yourself someplace far away. You may be on a
beach just before a storm, in a crowded marketplace in
a foreign country, or traveling down a river on a raft. On
the lines below, write a short paragraph describing what
you see. Use at least two similes in your paragraph.

_____

_____

_____

_____

## Lesson 3.20  Metaphors

Like a simile, a **metaphor** is a figure of speech that can be used to make a piece of writing more interesting. Use a metaphor to make a comparison without using the words *like* or *as*.

> Alejandro's short hair was **a small, sleek cap** perched on his head.
> Mrs. Gallo is **a mother hen** to all the children in the neighborhood.
> The students were **busy bees** as they prepared for the guest's arrival.

### Identify It

Read each sentence below. If it contains a simile, circle it and write **S** on the line. If it contains a metaphor, circle it and write **M** on the line.

1. _____ The fireflies were tiny stars in the dark blue sky.

2. _____ Worry filled the room like a cloud of smoke.

3. _____ The crickets were talented musicians that filled the night with music.

4. _____ The summer air smelled as sweet as cotton candy.

5. _____ Terrance's fingers were rubber as he desperately worked to untie the knots.

6. _____ The exhausted boy was a robot as he slowly made his way up the stairs to bed.

7. _____ The waves were like wild animals as they leaped at the expert surfer.

8. _____ Excitement was an electric current that ran through the stadium.

9. _____ Chelsea's eyes are as blue as the inside of the McIntyres' pool.

# Lesson 3.20 Metaphors

## Complete It

Read each metaphor below. Then, fill in the lines to show which two things are being compared.

Example: To Eli, the shrieking sirens were fingernails on a chalkboard.

_____shrieking sirens_____ compared to _____fingernails on a chalkboard_____

1. The falling leaves were confetti swirling in the air.

_____ compared to _____

2. The soap bubbles were pearls scattered along the edge of the tub.

_____ compared to _____

3. The tornado was a dinosaur that roared terribly at anything in its path.

_____ compared to _____

4. Although the air was cold, the sunlight was a blanket that warmed the cold children.

_____ compared to _____

5. The train was a bullet that shot through the tunnel at more than 70 miles an hour.

_____ compared to _____

## Try It

On the lines below, write two metaphors. You can begin your sentences with ideas from the box, or you can use ideas of your own.

| The thunderstorm was | The morning sun is | The tiny kitten was |
| --- | --- | --- |

1. _____

2. _____

# Lesson 3.21 | Personification

**Personification** means *to give human qualities to animals or objects.* Like other figures of speech, using personification in writing can make it more lively and interesting.

> The water flowed over the small stones in the creek.
> *The water **skipped and danced** over the small stones in the creek.*

> The old car came to a stop and didn't move.
> *The old car came to a stop and **stubbornly refused** to move.*

> It was tempting to eat the last piece of chocolate cake.
> *The last piece of chocolate cake **smiled and motioned** for me to come closer.*

## Identify It

Read each sentence below. Underline the part or parts of the sentence that show the writer is personifying an animal or a nonliving thing.

1. The bright yellow flowers drooped lazily in the afternoon heat.

2. The mouse adjusted his hat and bow tie, grabbed his briefcase, and kissed his wife on her downy cheek.

3. The fat pumpkin sat on the porch step and grinned cheerfully at the passing children.

4. "I have had nothing but canned food for three days," meowed Lola, "and I think it's time for a little fresh fish."

5. The wind pounded against the doors and windows, begging to come inside.

6. The spider glared angrily at the man who had just accidentally walked through her web.

## Lesson 3.21 Personification

**Rewrite It**

Rewrite each sentence below using personification. You may add or remove details from the sentences as needed.

I. Min flicked the switch and the computer came on.

_____

2. Streaks of lightning lit up the sky.

_____

3. The goldfish swam in circles in its bowl.

_____

4. The hurricane was quickly approaching land.

_____

5. The tiny green lizard scurried across the sidewalk.

_____

6. The bedside alarm rang loudly.

_____

**Try It**

On a separate sheet of paper, make a list of three animals, objects, or natural events. Then, write three sentences using personification to describe the items on your list.

_____

_____

_____

## Lesson 3.22 Using Descriptive Language

Good writers use **descriptive language** in their writing. A variety of adjectives and adverbs make details and descriptions richer. Using vivid verbs in place of common verbs adds interest to a piece of writing.

> Melita put the tomatoes in the basket.
> Melita *gingerly* placed the *sun-warmed* tomatoes in the *old wicker* basket.

> The cat walked across the room.
> The *tiny, pale gray* kitten *scampered* across the dining room's *slick wood* floors.

Sometimes, even changing or adding a single word can make a sentence more interesting.

> The news made Britta unhappy.    The news made Britta *miserable*.

**Identify It**

Read each pair of sentences below. Underline the sentence that makes better use of descriptive words.

1. Sally smiled at the class.
   Sally beamed at the class.

2. The weary baby wailed when she lost her favorite blanket.
   The small baby cried when she lost her blanket.

3. The large bumblebee flew over the pretty flowers.
   The fat, striped bumblebee hovered over the bright red tulips.

4. Andrew clomped down the stairs wearing his stiff new shoes.
   Andrew walked down the stairs wearing his shoes.

5. The Chinese food tasted both sweet and spicy to Xavier.
   The food they had for dinner tasted pretty good to Xavier.

## Lesson 3.22 Using Descriptive Language

### Rewrite It

Rewrite the phrases below. Add or substitute words to make each phrase more detailed or interesting.

Examples: the tall, old tree _____ the towering, ancient tree _____

closed the door _____ angrily slammed the door _____

1. climbed up the hill _____

2. the pony in the barnyard _____

3. the birds chirped _____

4. the gardener's hands _____

5. walked across the yard _____

6. the girl wearing a raincoat _____

7. smelled good _____

### Try It

Write a short paragraph that describes a special day you had, a favorite place, or a scary experience. Use descriptive words in your writing. Do not use common, generic words (like *nice, bad, big, tall*) if you can use specific words instead.

_____

_____

_____

_____

# Review Similes, Metaphors, Personification, and Descriptive Language

Using figurative language in your writing can make it more vivid and interesting.

A **simile** compares two unlike things using the words *like* or *as*.

> Heidi's lips were **as red as cherries**.

A **metaphor** is a comparison without using the words *like* or *as*.

> The tree was **an enormous umbrella**, shading us from the sun.

**Personification** is giving human qualities to things that are not human, like animals, objects, or natural events.

> The gentle breeze **whispered secrets** to Gemma.

Using **descriptive language** also adds life to a piece of writing. Try to use colorful, descriptive words and include a variety of adjectives and adverbs.

> There was a nice view of the mountains from the window.
> There was a *spectacular* view of the *lush, green* mountains from the window.

Also, remember to use verbs that provide a strong picture of the action. For example, instead of *run*, you could use *scamper, race, dash, sprint,* or *scramble*.

## Putting It Together

Read each sentence below. Write **S** if it contains a simile, **M** if it contains a metaphor, and **P** if it contains personification.

1. _____ The dry, parched earth of the desert waited patiently but eagerly for rain.

2. _____ The giant cactus was as tall and dignified as a soldier.

3. _____ The clouds were fluffy, white cotton balls scattered across the bright blue sky.

4. _____ The dry leaves skittered across the sand like tiny lizards.

# Review Similes, Metaphors, Personification, and Descriptive Language

For each item below, write a sentence using a figure of speech as shown in parentheses.

1. ocean water (simile)

   _____

2. a full moon (metaphor)

   _____

3. the small black ant (personification)

   _____

4. the sounds of nighttime (metaphor)

   _____

5. a slice of cold watermelon (simile)

   _____

Read each pair of sentences below. Circle the letter of the choice that makes better use of descriptive language.

1. **a.** I was happy to see him.    **b.** I was delighted to see him.

2. **a.** Ravi's voice was hoarse and raspy.    **b.** Ravi had a sore throat.

3. **a.** Shawn's hands were sticky and greasy.
   **b.** Shawn's hands were dirty.

4. **a.** It was going to be a cloudy day.
   **b.** It was going to be a damp, gloomy day.

5. **a.** We heard the birds in the nest.
   **b.** We heard the birds coo and chirp in the nest.

# Chapter 4
## Lesson 4.1  Writer's Guide: Prewriting

The five steps of the writing process are **prewriting**, **drafting**, **revising**, **proofreading**, and **publishing**.

**Prewriting**, the first stage of the writing process, involves planning and organizing. This is the stage where you get the ideas for your paper and start plotting it out.

When you prewrite, you:

- Think of ideas for your topic that are not too narrow or too broad. Write down your chosen ideas.

- Select your favorite topic, the one you think you can write about the best.

- Write down anything that comes to your mind about your chosen topic. Don't worry about grammar and spelling at this stage. This is called *freewriting*.

- Organize your information the way you might organize it in your paper. Use a graphic organizer. Graphic organizers visually represent the layout and ideas for a written paper. Graphic organizers include spider maps, Venn diagrams, story boards, network trees, and outlines.

- Use your graphic organizer to find out what information you already know and what information you need to learn more about.

**Prewriting Example**

Assignment: biography of a hero

Topic ideas: Martin Luther King, Jr., Eleanor Roosevelt, Jesse Owens, Cleveland Amory, Lance Armstrong, Rachel Carson

Freewriting of selected topic: Cleveland Amory hero of animals. Author.  Founder of the Fund for Animals. Wrote The Cat Who Came for Christmas. Read Black Beauty as a child and wanted a ranch for rescued animals. Established Black Beauty Ranch for rescued animals.

Graphic organizer:

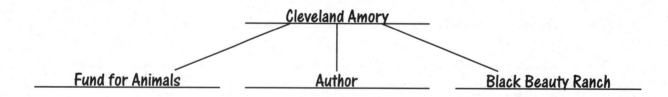

# Lesson 4.2  Writer's Guide: Drafting

**Drafting** involves writing your rough draft. Don't worry too much about grammar and spelling. Write down all of your thoughts about the subject, based on the structure of your graphic organizer.

When you draft, you:

- Write an **introduction** with a topic sentence. Get your readers' attention by stating a startling statistic or asking a question. Explain the purpose of your writing.

- Write the **body** of your paper. Use your graphic organizer to decide how many paragraphs will be included in your paper. Write one paragraph for each idea.

- Write your **conclusion**. Your conclusion will summarize your paper.

## Drafting Example

My hero was a hero: a hero to animals. Cleveland Amory (1917-1998) was an author, an animal advocate, and an animal rescuer. Reading Black Beauty as a child inspired a dream for Amory. Cleveland Amory made his dream a reality.

Amory founded The Fund for Animals. The Fund for Animals is an animal advocacy group that campaigns for animal protection. Amory served as its president, without pay, until his death in 1998. Cleveland Amory was an editor. He was an editor for The Saturday Evening Post. He served in World War II. After world war II, he wrote history books that studied society. He was a commentator on The Today Show, a critic for TV guide, a columnist for Saturday Review. Amory especially loved his own cat, Polar Bear, who inspired him to write three instant best-selling books: The Cat Who Came for Christmas, The Cat and the Curmudgeon, and The Best Cat Ever.

When Amory read Black Beauty as a child. When he read Black Beauty, he dreamed of place where animals could roam free and live in caring conditions. The dream is real at Black Beauty Ranch, a sanctuary for abused and abandoned animals The ranch's 1,620 acres serve as home for hundreds of animals, including elephants, horses, burros, ostriches, chimpanzees, and many more. Black Beauty Ranch takes in unwanted, abused, neglected, abandoned, and rescued domestic and exotic animals.

Cleveland Amory is my hero because he is a hero. He worked to make his dreams realities. His best-selling books, the founding of The Fund for Animals, and the opening of Black Beauty Ranch are the legacy of his dreams. Words from Anna Sewell's Black Beauty, the words that inspired Cleveland Amory, are engraved at the entrance to Black Beauty Ranch: "I have nothing to fear; and here my story ends. My troubles are all over, and I am at home." Cleveland Amory died on October 15, 1998. He is buried at Black Beauty Ranch, next to his beloved cat, Polar Bear.

## Lesson 4.3 Writer's Guide: Revising

**Revising** is the time to stop and think about what you have already written. It is time to rewrite.

When you revise, you:

- Add or change words.
- Delete unnecessary words or phrases.
- Move text around.
- Improve the overall flow of your paper.

**Revising Example (body of paper)**

Cleveland Amory did more than just write about the animals he loved.
Amory founded The Fund for Animals. (in 1967) The Fund for Animals is (one of the world's most active) an animal advocacy
group that campaigns for animal protection. (rights and) Amory served as its president, without
Amory extended his devotion to animals with Black Beauty Ranch
pay, until his death in 1998. Cleveland Amory was an editor. (started his writing career as) He was an editor for The
Saturday Evening Post. He served in World War II. After (serving in) world war II, he wrote history

books that studied society. He was a commentator on The Today Show, a critic for TV
Amory's love of animals, as well as great affection for
guide, a columnist for Saturday Review. Amory especially loved his own cat, Polar Bear,
led
who inspired him to write three instant best-selling books: The Cat Who Came for

Christmas, The Cat and the Curmudgeon, and The Best Cat Ever.

Cleveland Amory made his childhood dream come true in 1979 when he
opened Black Beauty Ranch in Texas.
When Amory read Black Beauty as a child. When he read Black Beauty, he

dreamed of place where animals could roam free and live in caring conditions. The
for hundreds of
dream is real at Black Beauty Ranch, a sanctuary for abused and abandoned animals

The ranch's 1,620 acres serve as home for hundreds of animals, including elephants,
animals
horses, burros, ostriches, chimpanzees, and many more. Black Beauty Ranch takes in

unwanted, abused, neglected, abandoned, and rescued domestic and exotic

animals.

# Lesson 4.4  Writer's Guide: Proofreading

**Proofreading** is the time to look for more technical errors.

When you proofread, you:

- Check spelling.
- Check grammar.
- Check punctuation.

**Proofreading Example (body of paper after revision)**

Cleveland Amory started his writing career as an editor for <u>The Saturday Evening</u>
<u>Post</u>. After serving in ẉorld ẉar II, he wrote history books that studied society. He was a
commentator on <u>The Today Show</u>, a critic for <u>TV g̲uide</u> ,^and a columnist for <u>Saturday</u>
<u>Review</u>. Amory's love of animals, as well as great affection for his own cat, Polar Bear,
led him to three instant best-selling books: <u>The Cat Who Came for Christmas</u>, <u>The Cat</u>
<u>and the Curmudgeon</u>, and <u>The Best Cat Ever</u>.

Cleveland Amory did more than just write about the animals he loved. Amory
founded The Fund for Animals in 1967. The Fund for Animals is one of the world's most
active animal advocacy group^s that campaigns for animal rights and protection.
Amory served as its president, without pay, until his death in 1998. Amory extended his
devotion to animals with Black Beauty Ranch.

Cleveland Amory made his childhood dream come true in 1979 when he opened
Black Beauty Ranch in Texas. He dreamed of^a place where animals could roam free
and live in caring conditions. The dream is real for hundreds of unwanted, abused,
neglected, abandoned, and rescued domestic and exotic animals at Black Beauty
Ranch.^o The ranch's 1,620 acres serve as home for elephants, horses, burros, ostriches,
chimpanzees, and many more animals.

## Lesson 4.5  Writer's Guide: Publishing

**Publishing** is the fifth and final stage of the writing process. Write your final copy and decide how you want to publish your work. Here is a list of some ideas:

- Read your paper to family and classmates.
- Illustrate and hang class papers in a "Hall of Fame" in your class or school.
- Publish your work in a school or community newspaper or magazine.

**Publishing (compare to the other three versions to see how it has improved)**

Biography of a Hero: Cleveland Amory

My hero was a hero: a hero to animals. Cleveland Amory (1917-1998) was an author, an animal advocate, and an animal rescuer. Reading <u>Black Beauty</u> as a child inspired a dream for Amory. Cleveland Amory made his dream a reality.

Cleveland Amory started his writing career as an editor for <u>The Saturday Evening Post</u>. After serving in World War II, Amory wrote history books that studied society. He was a commentator on <u>The Today Show</u>, a critic for <u>TV Guide</u>, and a columnist for <u>Saturday Review</u>. Amory's love of animals, as well as great affection for his own cat Polar Bear, led him to three instant best-selling books: <u>The Cat Who Came for Christmas</u>, <u>The Cat and the Curmudgeon</u>, and <u>The Best Cat Ever</u>.

Cleveland Amory did more than just write about the animals he loved. Amory founded The Fund for Animals in 1967. The Fund for Animals is one of the world's most active animal advocacy groups that campaigns for animal rights and protection. Amory served as its president, without pay, until his death in 1998. Amory extended his devotion to animals with Black Beauty Ranch.

Cleveland Amory made his childhood dream come true in 1979 when he opened Black Beauty Ranch in Texas. He dreamed of a place where animals could roam free and live in caring conditions. The dream is real for hundreds of unwanted, abused, neglected, abandoned, and rescued domestic and exotic animals at Black Beauty Ranch. The ranch's 1,620 acres serve as home for elephants, horses, burros, ostriches, chimpanzees, and many more animals.

Cleveland Amory is my hero because he is a hero. He worked to make his dreams realities. His best-selling books, the founding of The Fund for Animals, and the opening of Black Beauty Ranch are the legacy of his dreams. Words from Anna Sewell's <u>Black Beauty</u>, the words that inspired Cleveland Amory, are engraved at the entrance to Black Beauty Ranch: "I have nothing to fear; and here my story ends. My troubles are all over, and I am at home." Cleveland Amory died on October 15, 1998. He is buried at Black Beauty Ranch, next to his beloved cat, Polar Bear.

# Lesson 4.6 Writer's Guide: Evaluating Writing

When you are evaluating your own writing and the writing of others, being a critic is a good thing.

You can learn a lot about how you write by reading and rereading papers you have written. As you continue to write, your techniques will improve. You can look at previous papers and evaluate them. How would you change them to improve them knowing what you know now?

You can also look at the writing of others: classmates, school reporters, newspaper and magazine writers, and authors. Evaluate their writing, too. You can learn about different styles from reading a variety of written works. Be critical with their writing. How would you improve it?

Take the points covered in the Writer's Guide and make a checklist. You can use this checklist to evaluate your writing and others' writing, too. Add other items to the checklist as you come across them or think of them.

**Evaluation Checklist**

❑ Write an introduction with a topic sentence that will get your readers' attention. Explain the purpose of your writing.

❑ Write the body with one paragraph for each idea.

❑ Write a conclusion that summarizes the paper, stating the main points.

❑ Add or change words.

❑ Delete unnecessary words or phrases.

❑ Move text around.

❑ Improve the overall flow of your paper.

❑ Check spelling.

❑ Check grammar.

❑ Check punctuation.

❑ _____

❑ _____

❑ _____

NAME _____

## Lesson 4.7 Writer's Guide: Writing Process Practice

The following pages may be used to practice the writing process.

**Prewriting**

Assignment: _____

_____

Topic ideas: _____

_____

_____

Freewriting of selected topic: _____

_____

_____

_____

_____

_____

_____

_____

_____

_____

_____

_____

_____

Graphic Organizer:

## Lesson 4.7  Writer's Guide: Writing Process Practice

**Drafting**

_____
_____
_____
_____
_____
_____
_____
_____
_____
_____
_____
_____
_____
_____
_____
_____
_____
_____
_____
_____
_____
_____
_____
_____
_____
_____

# Lesson 4.7  Writer's Guide: Writing Process Practice

**Revising**

_____

_____

_____

_____

_____

_____

_____

_____

_____

_____

_____

_____

_____

_____

_____

_____

_____

_____

_____

_____

_____

_____

_____

_____

_____

_____

## Lesson 4.7  Writer's Guide: Writing Process Practice

**Proofreading**

_____
_____
_____
_____
_____
_____
_____
_____
_____
_____
_____
_____
_____
_____
_____
_____
_____
_____
_____
_____
_____
_____
_____
_____
_____
_____
_____
_____
_____
_____

## Lesson 4.7 Writer's Guide: Writing Process Practice

**Publishing**

**Final Draft: Include illustrations, photographs, graphic aids, etc.**

_____

_____

_____

_____

_____

_____

_____

_____

_____

_____

_____

_____

_____

_____

_____

_____

_____

_____

_____

_____

_____

_____

_____

_____

# Answer Key

**Common nouns** name people, places, things, and ideas.
> People: teacher, lawyer, baby, uncle, artist, girl, teenager, athlete
> Places: school, museum, library, kitchen, store, park
> Things: walnut, daffodil, opossum, fence, radio, cottage
> Ideas: bravery, fear, happiness, attitude, enthusiasm

**Proper nouns** name specific people, places, and things. Proper nouns are capitalized.
> People: Mandy Lopez, Alex, Aunt Kathleen, Mr. Reichman
> Places: Argentina, Windgate Elementary School, Philadelphia Zoo
> Things: Timber City County Fair

**Tip** Some nouns are made up of more than a single word: life jacket, polar bear, University of Iowa, Museum of Science and Technology.

## Complete It
Fill in the blanks in the chart below with the missing common or proper nouns. You may use real or fictional proper nouns.

Example: President — George Washington

| Common Nouns | Proper Nouns |
|---|---|
| teacher | ____ |
| ____ | Duke University |
| singer | |
| father | *Answers will vary.* |
| ____ | Bixby Memorial Library |
| | Mississippi |
| team | ____ |

**6**

---

## Identify It
Read the following paragraphs. Underline the 22 common nouns. Circle the 14 proper nouns. Remember that a noun can sometimes be more than one word.

The (National Museum of American History) is located in (Washington, D.C.) It is run by the (Smithsonian Institution). The museum is full of many interesting things. On the second floor, you can see clothes and other items that belonged to (First Ladies) Dresses that were worn by (Dolley Madison) and (Nancy Reagan) are displayed. You can also see famous flags of the (United States.) One flag hung over (Fort McHenry) during the (War of 1812.)

The museum owns many amazing pieces of history. They own a watch that belonged to (Helen Keller) a top hat that belonged to (Abraham Lincoln,) and boxing gloves that were used by (Muhammad Ali.) You can send a message by telegraph, or check out the ruby slippers worn by (Dorothy) in the movie (The Wizard of Oz.) Excitement builds as you realize how many things there are to do and see. Plan to visit the museum for more than one day.

## Try It
1. Write a sentence about three things you might see in an art museum. Underline the common nouns.

   *Answers will vary.*

2. Write a sentence about a person you would like to interview or a place you would like to visit. Circle the proper nouns.

   *Answers will vary.*

**7**

---

A **pronoun** is a word that stands for a noun. Using pronouns helps you avoid repeating the same nouns in your writing.

Some pronouns, like *I, me, you, he, she, him, her,* and *it*, refer to a single person or thing. Other pronouns, like *we, us, they,* and *them*, refer to plural nouns.

| | |
|---|---|
| Carter and Jess belong to the tennis club. | *They* belong to the tennis club. |
| The cashier handed the *change* to Melissa. | The cashier handed *it* to *her*. |
| Vijay lives two blocks away. | *He* lives two blocks away. |

**Possessive pronouns** are pronouns that show ownership. *My, your, his, her, its, our,* and *their* are all examples of possessive pronouns.
> *my* jacket   *your* sister   *our* car   *his* dog   *their* ideas

## Complete It
Complete the second sentence in each pair with the missing pronoun or pronouns.

1. Ms. Rittenhouse assigned a report to the students in our science class.

   __She__ wanted us to research people __we__ admire.

2. Harry wrote a biography of Charles Henry Turner.

   When Harry grows up, __he__ hopes to become a scientist, too.

3. Charles Henry Turner spent many hours observing insects.

   __His__ research proved that bugs can hear.

4. Aliya's report was on Margaret Mead, who studied how the people in other cultures live.

   I think __her__ report was one of the most interesting.

**8**

---

## Identify It
Read the following paragraphs. Find and circle the 19 pronouns.

(I) am writing a report about Dr. Mae Jemison for (my) science class (She) was the first African American woman to travel into space. In 1992, Mae was aboard the space shuttle *Endeavor* on (its) eight-day journey (I) first learned about Mae Jemison from (my) dad (He) is an engineer at NASA. (He) met Mae at an awards ceremony a long time ago.

(I) think that Mae Jemison is an amazing person because of (her) determination. (She) graduated from high school and began college when (she) was only 16 years old. After going to medical school, Mae spent some time working in countries like Cuba, Kenya, and Thailand.

(It) was not easy for Mae to achieve (her) dreams (She) worked hard and never gave up. Today (she) is glad to be a role model for girls all over the world. (They) can look at Mae Jemison's accomplishments and know that nothing can stop (them) from reaching (their) goals.

## Try It
Write two sentences about someone you admire. Use at least one pronoun and one possessive pronoun in your sentences. Circle the pronouns.

*Answers will vary.*

**9**

---

Spectrum Language Arts
Grade 4

Answer Key
**163**

---

**Verbs** tell what happens in a sentence. Many verbs are action words. They tell what the subject of the sentence does.

> Emilio carefully *opened* the can.
> He *dipped* the brush in the paint and *swirled* it around.

**Solve It**

Write the verb or verbs from each sentence on the lines.

1. Madeleine sang "Yesterday" by the Beatles for the talent show.
   s (a) n g

2. Eddie practiced his knock-knock jokes and riddles for weeks before the show.
   (p) r a c t i c e d

3. Erica juggled oranges, eggs, golf balls, and beanbags.
   j u g g (l) e d

4. Vinh played two songs on the piano.
   p l a (y) e d

5. Ryan recited three poems from memory.
   (r) e c i t e d

6. Lily and Joel danced the tango, the waltz, and the rumba.
   d a n (c) e d

7. Miyako showed the crowd her best gymnastics moves.
   s h o w e (d)

8. Topher acted out a scene from The Wind in the Willows.
   a c t (e) d

Write the circled letters from your answers on the lines below.

a p l y r c d e

Unscramble the letters to find out what the grand prize was.

C D   p l a y e r

**10**

---

**Complete It**

Complete each of the following sentences with a verb. There may be more than one correct answer, but the verb you choose should make sense in the sentence.

1. More than one hundred people _____ to the talent show.

2. The performers _____ while the audience clapped.

3. The judges _____ they would have a difficult decision to make.

4. While Erica was juggling, she accidentally _____ an egg.

5. Madeleine _____ ‾‾‾‾ en she was only five years old.

6. Last year, Joel _____ his ankle while he was dancing.

7. Miyako's sister _____ the grand prize at the talent show when she was ten.

8. After the show, the parents and the performers drank punch and _____ cookies.

> Answers will vary.

**Try It**

Write a short paragraph about what you and your friends would do if your school had a talent show. Circle the verbs in your paragraph.

_____

_____

> Answers will vary.

_____

_____

**11**

---

A **helping verb** works with the main verb in a sentence. It always comes before the main verb. When words like *am, is, are, was, were, has, have, had,* and *will* are used with a main verb in a sentence, they are helping verbs.

> Marty **is** *going* to the dentist tomorrow morning.
> The creek **will** *flood* from the heavy rains.
> Samantha **has** *read* that book many times.
> The squirrel **was** *hiding* nuts in the backyard.

**Identify It**

In the sentences below, circle the helping verbs. Underline the main verbs.

1. The first bicycles (were) invented in the early 1800s.

2. An early type of bicycle (was) called a *boneshaker*.

3. Many people (have) contributed to the development of the modern bicycle.

4. Some bicycles (were) built for two people.

5. Today, postal workers, police officers, and delivery people (are) using bicycles at work.

6. My family (is) joining the Ashview Cycling Club.

7. We (are) planning a weekend trip to some nearby rail-trails.

8. We (will) ride about ten miles each day.

| Tip | Another word can sometimes come between a helping verb and a main verb. Read carefully to be sure you identify both parts of the verb. The baby *has* often *dropped* her pacifier under the table. The Crenshaws *will* probably *come* to dinner on Saturday. |
| --- | --- |

**12**

---

**Complete It**

Read the paragraphs below. Fill in each space with a helping verb from the box. You may use some helping verbs more than once.

| is | are | have |
| --- | --- | --- |
| will | had | were |

There are many different kinds of bicycles available today. Deciding how you _____ use your bicycle is an important first step. Mountain bikes _____ designed for off-road biking. They _____ used for riding on unpaved roads and paths. People _____ used bicycles for racing since the late 1800s. Cyclists who _____ competing in a race today want a bike that is light and has many gears. In Europe, many people _____ ride _____ ong, sturdy, and practical. A person v_____ carrying a heavy load can depend on a utility bike for a smooth, inexpensive ride.

> Answers will vary.

Some bikes _____ carry more than one person at a time. Tandem bikes _____ built for two people. The largest bicycle ever ridden was a multi-bicycle. A string of 40 people rode it at the same time. If the lead cyclist _____ fallen, the rest of the bikers would _____ been in a lot of trouble!

**Try It**

Write two sentences. Each sentence should have a helping verb and a main verb. Circle the helping verb, and underline the main verb.

1. _____

2. _____

> Answers will vary.

**13**

---

---

**Linking verbs** link, or connect, the subject of a sentence to the rest of the sentence. The verb *to be* can be a linking verb. Some different forms of the verb *to be* are *is, am, are, was,* and *were. Become, feel, seem, look, appear, taste, smell,* and *sound* are also linking verbs.

Jefferson City *is* the capital of Missouri.

Jackie Robinson *was* the first African-American baseball player in the major leagues.

Stephen Hawking *became* famous for his study of black holes.

As you learned in the last lesson, *is, am, are, was,* and *were* are **helping verbs** when they are used with the main verb in a sentence. When these verbs are used alone, they are **linking verbs**.

(helping verb) (main verb)          (linking verb)

Ms. Bernstein *is helping* us.     Ms. Bernstein *is* my teacher.

**Identify It**

In each sentence below, underline the verb. If it is a linking verb, write **LV** on the line. If it is a helping verb that is used with a main verb, write **HV**.

1. __HV__ Roald Dahl's first book <u>was published</u> in 1966.

2. __LV__ He <u>was</u> the author of popular books like <u>The BFG</u>, <u>Matilda</u>, and <u>James and the Giant Peach</u>.

3. __LV__ Roald <u>became</u> friends with Franklin and Eleanor Roosevelt.

4. __LV__ He <u>appeared</u> funny, kind, and intelligent to fans and readers of all ages.

5. __HV__ Roald Dahl's children <u>were named</u> Olivia, Theo, Tessa, Ophelia, and Lucy.

6. __HV__ Today, his books <u>are loved</u> by children all around the world.

7. __LV__ Dahl's characters <u>become</u> real to readers of his books.

14

---

**Complete It**

Read the sentences below. Complete each sentence with a linking verb.

1. The book <u>A Cricket in Times Square</u> _____ by George Selden.

2. Selden _____ a famous children's book writer.

3. After reading <u>A Cricket in Times Square</u> many times, it _____ my favorite book.

4. Chester Cricket, _____ wonderful characters.

   [Answers will vary.]

5. I _____ like I know them because they _____ so real.

6. I _____ sure that almost any child or adult would enjoy this book.

**Try It**

Write a short paragraph about your favorite book. Use at least three linking verbs in your paragraph. Underline the linking verbs.

_____

_____

_____

   [Answers will vary.]

_____

_____

_____

15

---

**Putting It Together**

Rewrite each sentence below. Use a proper noun in place of each underlined common noun.

1. The <u>boy</u> was traveling to another <u>country</u> with his <u>uncle</u>.

_____

2. The <u>school</u> is o   [Answers will vary.]

_____

3. My <u>teacher</u> is taking our class to the <u>museum</u>.

_____

Read the sentences below. Circle the nouns. Underline the pronouns once. Underline the possessive pronouns twice.

1. The (photographer) flew to Africa and traveled to many countries.

2. <u>Her</u> (grandfather) gave <u>her</u> a (camera) when <u>she</u> graduated from (college.)

3. (Stella) photographed (animals) (villages) (children) and (landscapes)

Each of the sentences below is missing a verb. The words in parentheses will tell you what type of verb to use to complete the sentence.

1. Stella _____ a photographer. (linking verb)

2. She _____ never traveled to Afri___ before. (helping verb)

3. Stella's grandf[   Answers will vary.   ]e as much of the world as possible. (action verb)

4. He _____ that we can learn a lot by meeting people who live in faraway places. (action verb)

17

---

**Adjectives** are words that describe nouns or pronouns. Adjectives often answer the questions *What kind? How many?* and *Which one?* Good descriptive words help the reader form a picture in his or her mind.

*yellow* boots     *dangerous* journey     *this* plate     *several* students

An adjective may come before the word it describes, or it may follow the verb in a sentence.

The *roaring* fire made the room feel *warm* and *cozy*.

Isabella's *red* bathing suit stood out against the *pale* sand and the *crisp, blue* sky.

*Four spotted* toads sat on *mossy* logs beside the *shallow* pond.

**Identify It**

Read the diary entry below. There are 22 adjectives. Find and circle each adjective.

Saturday, September 2

Dear Diary,

Today was a (strange) day. I looked out the window (this) afternoon and knew a (big) storm was coming. The sky was (dark). A (thin,) (yellow) line stretched across the horizon. The air felt (sticky) and (thick.)

Suddenly, I heard a (loud) knocking on the ceiling and the windows. (Tiny) (icy) chunks of hail were falling from the (stormy) sky. When I looked out the window, I saw the hail bounce off the top of a (red) car, a (city) bus, and a (large) umbrella.

A minute later, the lights went out. Mom put (new) batteries in our flashlights, and she found some (old) candles in the (junk) drawer. We made (turkey) sandwiches and had a (candlelit) dinner. The lights came back on just in time for bed. The (heavy) rain had stopped, and I fell asleep to the (quiet) pitter-patter of raindrops on the roof of our building.

18

---

# Answer Key

---

**Rewrite It**

Rewrite the sentences below. Include at least one adjective to describe every underlined noun. Try to use adjectives that make the sentences as interesting and descriptive as you can.

Example: The bird sat in the tree.
___The cheerful red bird sat in the gnarled old tree.___

1. The girl put on her raincoat and boots.

2. After the snowstorm, the plows cleared the streets.

**Answers will vary.**

3. A rainbow appeared ~~in the sky~~ behind the house.

4. The farmer and his family took shelter from the tornado in the basement.

**Try It**

Write about an experience you have had with the weather. You might write about a thunderstorm, a snowstorm, a sunny day, or a drought. Use at least five adjectives in your paragraph. Circle the adjectives.

**Answers will vary.**

19

---

**Adverbs** are words that describe verbs, adjectives, and other adverbs. Many adverbs end with the letters **ly**. Adverbs often answer the questions *When? Where? How?* or *How much?*

Raymond *easily* sank the basketball. (*Easily* describes the verb *sank* by telling how.)
We were *too* late to see the movie. (*Too* describes the adjective *late* by telling how.)
Alicia should arrive *very soon*. (*Soon* describes the verb *arrive* by telling when. *Very* describes the adverb *soon* by telling how.)

To decide whether a word is an adverb, find the word it modifies, or describes. If it answers the questions *What kind? How many?* or *Which one?* the word is probably an adjective. If it tells *When? Where? How?* or *How much?* it is probably an adverb.

**Identify It**

Read the paragraphs below. Find and circle the 11 adverbs. Then, draw an arrow from each adverb to the word it modifies, or describes.

Earthworms should be welcomed (eagerly) into any garden. They eat soil and make tunnels. The worms digest the soil, and the waste material they leave (behind) is called *castings*. These castings are (extremely) good for the soil. They make it (very) rich in nutrients. The tunnels earthworms (patiently) dig are good for the soil. They allow oxygen and nutrients to travel (easily) to the plant's roots. Soil that is packed (loosely) allows water to drain (quickly).

Earthworms are amazing in many other ways, too. If a worm is (accidentally) cut in half by a shovel or a rake, it can grow a (completely) new back half! Worms are (incredibly) strong, too. A worm the size of a human being would be about 1,000 times stronger than that human!

20

---

**Solve It**

Underline the adverb or adverbs in each sentence. Then, search for the 11 adverbs in the word search puzzle. Circle each adverb you find in the puzzle.

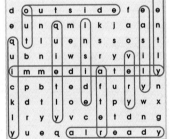

1. Your garden already has some earthworms, but you can easily add more.

2. Go outside at night, and bring a flashlight with you.

3. Walk very quietly so that you do not wake your neighbors.

4. If you find a worm inside its hole, gently dig it out.

5. If you go earthworm hunting immediately after a storm, you will quickly find many worms.

6. After you release the worms in your garden, the soil will become richer.

**Try It**

Imagine that you had a friend who had never seen a worm before. How would you describe it? Write several sentences that describe how worms look, feel, move, and so on. Use at least two adverbs in your description. Circle the adverbs.

**Answers will vary.**

21

---

An **article** is a word that comes before a noun. Use *the* to talk about a specific person, place, or thing. *The* can be used with a singular or plural noun.

*the* telescope    *the* orangutan    *the* goldfish    *the* skateboards

Use *a* or *an* to talk about any singular person, place, or thing. If the noun begins with a consonant sound, use *a*. If it begins with a vowel sound, use *an*.

*a* **p**illow    *a* **c**antaloupe    *an* **o**ctopus    *an* **e**arring

**Complete It**

Read the sentences below. Choose the correct article from the pair in parentheses to complete each sentence. Write it in the space.

1. Totem poles are made by Native American tribes of __the__ Pacific Northwest. (a, the)

2. __The__ colors that are most often used in the Northern style are red, black, and turquoise. (The, An)

3. A totem pole might tell __a__ family legend. (a, an)

4. Some poles tell the story of __an__ important event. (a, an)

5. It can take __an__ artist nine months to carve a totem pole. (an, a)

6. Many people think of a totem pole as __a__ piece of art. (an, a)

> **Tip**
> When deciding to use *a* or *an*, remember to pay attention to the sound at the beginning of a word, not just the first letter of the word. *Hour* begins with the consonant **h** but has a vowel sound **ow**. Use the article *an*—*an hour*. *Unit* begins with the vowel **u** but has a consonant sound **y**. Use the article *a*—*a unit*.

22

---

Spectrum Language Arts
Grade 4

166

Answer Key

## Proof It

Read the paragraphs below. Find and circle the 28 articles. Twelve of the articles are incorrect. Use proofreaders' marks to correct them.

| ℰ – delete |
| ^ – insert |

Totem poles can be (a) reminder of (an) family's history. (The) carved human and animal figures tell (the) story of (a) family's ancestors. Each animal has (the) special meaning to (an) tribe. (An) order of (the) animals on (the) pole is also important. (An) interpreter, or (a) expert in (an) culture, can help explain (the) meanings of (a) symbols. For example, (a) animal like (a) coyote can be (a) symbol of (a) trickster. (A) eagle represents courage or bravery. (A) bear is (a) caring figure.

Sadly, very few of (an) oldest totem poles still exist today. (A) weather in (the) Northwest is rainy and moist. Most totem poles have rotted after spending long years in (the) rain and wind. (The) few poles that have been saved can be viewed at museums like (a) Royal British Columbia Museum.

### Try It

1. Make a list of five animals or figures you would include if you made a totem pole. Be sure to use the correct article before each item.

> Answers will vary.

2. Write a sentence that includes all three articles.

> Answers will vary.

**23**

---

**Adjectives** describe nouns or pronouns and answer the questions *What kind? How many?* or *Which one?*
> The *sparkling* stars lit the *night* sky.
> The *enormous* watermelon was *cool* and *refreshing*.

**Adverbs** describe verbs, adjectives, and other adverbs. Adverbs often answer the questions *When? Where? How?* or *How much?*
> Alla *cheerfully* smiled for the camera.
> I will write you a letter *soon*.
> Jason was *too* tired to watch the end of the movie.

An **article** is a word that comes before a noun. *The* refers to a specific person, place, or thing. *A* or *an* refer to any person, place, or thing. Use *a* with words that begin with a consonant sound. Use *an* with words that begin with a vowel sound.
> *the* subway       *the* astronauts       *a* football       *an* **a**ccident

### Putting It Together

Fill in each space below with the correct article.

1. A firefighter is ___a___ person who is trained to put out fires and rescue people.

2. Firefighters try to take away ___the___ things a fire needs to burn: fuel, heat, and oxygen.

3. Sometimes water is used to put out ___a___ fire, and sometimes ___a___ type of foam is used.

4. In ___an___ emergency, firefighters must think and act quickly.

5. ___An___ alarm alerts firefighters that there is ___a___ fire.

6. It is important to test ___the___ batteries several times a year in a home fire alarm.

**24**

---

Read the sentences below. Circle the 12 adjectives you find. Underline the 7 adverbs.

1. Firefighting can be (exciting), but it is a (difficult) job.

2. The temperature (inside) (burning) buildings can be (extremely) (high).

3. (Experienced) firefighters can work (quickly) and (calmly).

4. They (often) work (long) shifts, so they spend (many) hours (together).

5. (These) (brave) men and women must be in (excellent) shape.

6. (Many) firefighters (proudly) say that they have the (best) job in the world.

Rewrite the sentences below. If *adj.* is at the end of the sentence, add an adjective to describe the underlined word. If *adv.* is at the end of the sentence, add an adverb to describe the underlined word.

1. The <u>fire engine</u> raced down the street. (*adj.*)

2. The firefighter <u>stepped</u> over the hose. (*adv.*)

3. The firehouse's D [Answers will vary.] nded. (*adv.*)

4. The <u>firefighter</u> put on his oxygen mask and nodded to his partner. (*adj.*)

**25**

---

A **preposition** is a word that connects a noun or a pronoun to another part of the sentence. Every preposition has an object. If you are not sure whether a word is a preposition, remember to look for its object.

Some common prepositions are *at, in, on, to, for, into, onto, with, under, over, before, during, after,* and *across.* In the examples below, the prepositions are in bold print. The objects are underlined.
> The tools are **in** <u>the basement</u>.
> The kiwis are **on** <u>the kitchen table</u>.
> Quinn and Ann are **at** <u>the movies</u>.
> Put away your bikes **before** <u>the storm</u>.
> Miguel waited **for** <u>three hours</u>.

### Identify It

In each sentence below, circle the preposition. Then, underline the object.

1. Yesterday was Pajama Day (at) <u>school</u>.

2. Terrell looked (in) <u>his dresser drawer</u>.

3. He decided to wear striped pajamas (for) <u>Pajama Day</u>.

4. He searched everywhere and finally found his slippers (under) <u>the bed</u>.

5. His sister, Erika, wore a bathrobe (over) <u>her pajamas</u>.

6. Terrell and Erika climbed (onto) <u>the bus</u> and laughed when they saw what their friends were wearing.

| Tip | The word *to* is not always a preposition. When *to* comes before a verb, it is part of the verb. |
| --- | --- |
| | prep.                                   verb |
| | I am going *to* the basketball game. I would like *to meet* your sister. |

**26**

# Answer Key

## Complete It

Complete the sentences below with prepositions from the box. Some prepositions may be used more than once.

| for | under | across | with | to |
|---|---|---|---|---|
| in | on | at | during | |

1. Ms. Molina wore curlers ___**in**___ her hair.

2. ___**At**___ lunchtime, the cafeteria served pancakes ___**with**___ eggs.

3. Terrell ate lunch ___**with**___ Michael, Antonio, Eliza, and Seeta.

4. Ms. Molina's students felt silly playing kickball ___**in**___ their pajamas ___**during**___ recess.

5. Terrell made it ___**to**___ third base when he kicked the ball ___**across**___ the field.

6. Jana and Maddy put their stuffed animals ___**on**___ their desks.

7. Two sixth graders took photos ___**for**___ the school newspaper.

8. Terrell's friend Michael dropped his toothbrush ___**under**___ his desk.

### Try It

Write a short paragraph about a special day or event at your school. Use at least four prepositions in your paragraph. Circle the prepositions.

> **Answers will vary.**

**27**

---

A **conjunction** is a connecting word. It can join words, sentences, or parts of sentences. Some common conjunctions are *and, or, but,* and *because.*

> Rachael *and* Colin rode the bus to the YMCA.
> Will the Bengals *or* the Broncos win the game?
> I like going to the pool, *but* I would rather swim at the beach.
> Kenji ran back inside the apartment *because* he forgot his lunch.

## Complete It

Read the advertisement below. Circle the conjunction in parentheses that best completes each sentence.

**VISIT HARBOR SPRINGS AMUSEMENT PARK!**

Do you like fast rides, (and (or)) would you rather test your game skills?

We have two new roller coasters, a wave pool, (or (and)) many activities for little ones.

Families come to Harbor Springs Park (or (because)) they know they'll have a great time.

We are not the biggest park in the state, (but) or) we are the best!

Children under five (because, (and)) senior citizens get in for free.

Visitors who arrive before 11 A.M. receive a free water bottle (and,) but) $2 off admission.

Hours: Monday–Thursday 9:30 A.M.–10 P.M.

Friday, Saturday, (and) or) Sunday 9 A.M.–11 P.M.

**28**

---

## Identify It

Read the letter below. Find and circle the 11 conjunctions.

July 14

Dear Haley,

Are you having a good summer? I can't believe it's already July, (but) I am glad there is still another month of vacation left. Last weekend, Eva, Dad, (and) I went to Harbor Springs Amusement Park. The park was crowded (because) it was such a nice day. Eva (and) Dad loved a roller coaster called "the Quicksilver," (but) I liked the Ferris wheel best. I rode it four times. I would have kept going, (but) it was time for lunch.

I think I like Ferris wheels (because) you can see so far when you reach the top. Did you know that the first Ferris wheel carried 2,160 people (and) weighed 2,200 tons? I wish I could take a ride on it, (but) it was built for the World's Fair in 1893. Maybe someday I can go to Japan (and) ride the Sky Dream Fukuoka. It is one of the biggest Ferris wheels in the world.

Write back to me (or) call soon. I can't wait to see you in August!

Your best friend,

Lola

### Try It

If you could invent an amusement park ride, what would it be like? Describe your ride using at least two conjunctions in your answer.

> **Answers will vary.**

**29**

---

A **preposition** connects a noun or a pronoun to another part of the sentence. *At, in, on, to, for, into, onto, with, under, over, before, during, after,* and *across* are prepositions. To be sure a word is a preposition, look for its object in the sentence.

> Jonathan played a board game *with* his parents *on* Saturday night.
> The coach gave the players a pep talk *before* the game.
> Ellie ran *across* the yard and jumped *in* the pool.

A **conjunction** joins words, sentences, or parts of sentences. *And, or, but,* and *because* are common conjunctions.

> Ms. Cree loves strawberries, *but* she is allergic to them.
> Will *and* Amber sat on the porch *because* it was hot inside.

### Putting It Together

Read the sentences below. If the underlined word is a preposition, write *prep.* on the line. If it is a conjunction, write *conj.* on the line.

1. __**prep.**__ The Iditarod is a sled-dog race <u>across</u> Alaska.

2. __**conj.**__ The mushers <u>and</u> their teams of dogs must be ready for all kinds of conditions.

3. __**prep.**__ They race <u>from</u> Anchorage to Nome.

4. __**prep.**__ The first Iditarod was held <u>in</u> 1973.

5. __**conj.**__ Thirty-five mushers entered the race, <u>but</u> thirteen of them did not finish.

6. __**conj.**__ Most mushers use Alaskan huskies <u>because</u> they are strong and hardworking.

7. __**prep.**__ <u>After</u> a race, the mushers and their dogs are eager to relax and get warm.

**30**

## Page 31

Read the paragraphs below. Circle the nine conjunctions. Underline the 19 prepositions.

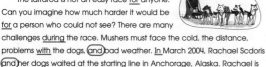

The Iditarod is not an easy race <u>for</u> anyone. Can you imagine how much harder it would be <u>for</u> a person who could not see? There are many challenges <u>during</u> the race. Mushers must face the cold, the distance, problems <u>with</u> the dogs, (and) bad weather. <u>In</u> March 2004, Rachael Scdoris (and) her dogs waited <u>at</u> the starting line <u>in</u> Anchorage, Alaska. Rachael is blind, (but) she knows she can do anything she wants. She just has to work a little harder sometimes.

Rachael's guide, Paul, was always <u>in</u> touch <u>with</u> her <u>by</u> radio. He gave her directions <u>for</u> leading the team <u>over</u> a hill (or) <u>under</u> a bank <u>of</u> trees. Rachael raced <u>for</u> 750 miles. Then, she made the hard decision to quit, (or) *scratch*, 400 miles <u>from</u> the finish line. Five <u>of</u> her dogs were sick (and) were losing weight. Rachael knew that the health <u>of</u> her dogs was more important than the race.

Rachael is the first blind musher to try to run the Iditarod, (but) she doesn't want to be remembered (because) she is blind. Rachael wants to be remembered (because) she is a good athlete <u>with</u> a big heart.

In each sentence below, circle the preposition. Then, underline the object.

1. Rachael Scdoris was born (in) <u>Oregon</u>.
2. She carried the torch (to) <u>the Salt Lake City Winter Olympics</u>.
3. Rachael feels a strong bond (with) <u>her dogs</u>.
4. The dogs pull the sled quickly (across) <u>the frozen ground</u>.

**31**

## Page 32

A **declarative sentence** is a statement. It begins with a capital letter and ends with a period. A statement gives information.
> **K**yra and Whitney are twins.  **C**han's painting is not dry yet.
> **M**aine is well known for its lobster.

An **imperative sentence** is a command. Use a command to request something. A command also begins with a capital letter and ends with a period.
> **D**on't forget to bring the bag.  **P**ut the bread on the counter.
> **L**eave your umbrella in the hallway.
> **R**ead the first two pages.

**Identify It**
Read each sentence below. Write **D** in the space if it is a declarative sentence. Write **I** if it is an imperative sentence.

1. __D__ Pizza is a favorite food all around the world.
2. __I__ Make your own pizza at home with just a few ingredients.
3. __D__ You can use pita bread or an English muffin for the crust.
4. __I__ Have an adult chop vegetables like peppers and olives.
5. __I__ Spread some tomato sauce on the bread, and add your toppings.
6. __D__ Most people use mozzarella cheese, but some like provolone.
7. __I__ Sprinkle the cheese on top of your pizza, and bake it until the topping is bubbly.

| Tip | **Statements** usually begin with a noun or a pronoun. *The characters* in my favorite book are named Milo and Flannery. **Commands** often begin with a verb. *Look* at the rabbit hiding in the bushes. |
|---|---|

**32**

## Page 33

**Proof It**
Some of the sentences in the paragraphs below are missing periods. Use proofreaders' marks to add the missing periods. Then, find the two imperative sentences and underline them.

⊙ – insert period

Pizzas have a long history in Europe⊙ The first written history of Rome, from 300 B.C., had a description of a flat bread with olive oil, herbs, and other toppings. The first pizzeria was in Naples, Italy⊙ It opened in 1830 and is still in business today! <u>Visit this shop for a taste of a real Italian pie⊙</u>

In 1905, an Italian immigrant opened the first pizza shop in America. It was called Lombardis⊙ The shop was located in New York City. The pizza was popular, but most of the customers were other Italians⊙ It took a few decades for the rest of America to learn to love this hot, cheesy food.

By the 1950s, pizza chains started opening around the country⊙ Pizza could be made quickly and delivered to people's homes. Everyone loved the convenience. People also liked ordering a pizza just the way they wanted it⊙ <u>Order a pizza today, or make one of your own⊙</u> You will experience a little bit of food history with every bite⊙

**Try It**
1. Write a command you might find in a recipe for making pizza.

_____

2. Write a statement | Answers will vary. |

**33**

## Page 34

An **interrogative sentence** is a question. A person asks a question to find more information about something. An interrogative sentence begins with a capital letter and ends with a question mark.
> **D**id you take the subway**?**  **W**here will the new library be**?**
> **C**an we go canoeing on Saturday**?**

An **exclamatory sentence** shows excitement, surprise, or strong feelings. An exclamatory sentence begins with a capital letter and ends with an exclamation point.
> The dog got out!  There is a bug in your hair!
> The shuttle has to make an emergency landing!

Sometimes, an exclamation can be a single word. Sometimes, it can contain a command.
> Surprise!  Uh-oh!  Help!  Look out!  Play ball!  Come here!

**Complete It**
The sentences below are missing end marks. Add a question mark to the end of interrogative sentences. Add an exclamation point to the end of exclamatory sentences.

1. Have you ever heard of Roberto Clemente_?_
2. He was one of the best outfielders of all time_!_
3. Did Roberto play for any teams other than the Pittsburgh Pirates_?_
4. How many schools in the United States are named after Roberto Clemente_?_
5. "Clemente is the best_!_" shouted a fan after the Pirates beat the Orioles in the 1971 World Series.
6. Did you know that Roberto did a lot of charity work during the off-season_?_

**34**

# Answer Key

---

**Rewrite It**

Rewrite each sentence below. If there is an **I** after the sentence, rewrite it as an interrogative sentence. If there is an **E** after the sentence, rewrite it as an exclamatory sentence.

Example: Roberto Clemente was born on August 18, 1934. (I)
_When was Roberto Clemente born?_

1. Roberto Clemente was born in Carolina, Puerto Rico. (I)

2. He was elected to the National Baseball Hall of Fame in 1973. (I)

3. During his career, Roberto had 3,000 hits. (E)

   **Answers will vary.**

4. Roberto was only 38 years old when he died in a plane crash. (I)

5. He was on his way to help the victims of an earthquake in Nicaragua. (I)

6. He earned 12 Gold Glove awards in a row. (E)

**Try It**

Think of a famous athlete. Now, write two questions you would like to ask that athlete.

**Answers will vary.**

**35**

---

**Declarative sentences** and **imperative sentences** both begin with a capital letter and end with a period. A declarative sentence is a statement that gives information. An imperative sentence is used to give a command or request something.

| Declarative Sentences | Imperative Sentences |
|---|---|
| Male cardinals are bright red. | Answer the phone. |
| Lydia has curly brown hair. | Wear your new jeans. |

An interrogative sentence asks a question. It begins with a capital letter and ends with a question mark.

What is the capital of Georgia**?**    How old will Kent be this year**?**

An exclamatory sentence shows excitement, surprise, or strong feelings. It begins with a capital letter and ends with an exclamation point.

We need help!        Amina got a puppy today!

**Putting It Together**

Read each sentence below, and decide what type of sentence it is. Write **D** if it is a declarative sentence, **IMP** if it is an imperative sentence, **INT** if it is an interrogative sentence, and **E** if it is an exclamatory sentence.

1. __D__ The bus dropped off Hiroshi, Jacob, Teresa, and Grace at the community center.

2. __D__ The center was putting on a play.

3. __INT__ Have you ever heard of the play The Princess and the Pea?

4. __D__ Hiroshi and Grace hoped to get small roles, and Teresa tried out for the lead.

5. __IMP__ Look at the cast list on the bulletin board.

6. __E__ "I got the part!"

**36**

---

Read the sentences below. If the end mark is correct, make a check mark on the line. If the end mark is not correct, delete it ( ⌐ℯ ) and write the correct end mark on the line.

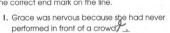

1. Grace was nervous because she had never performed in front of a crowd ~~?~~ .

2. Mrs. Wilmott asked, "Jacob, will you help paint the scenery for the play?" ✓

3. Jacob exclaimed, "I'd love to ~~?~~ _!_

4. Teresa wondered, "How many performances will there be?" ✓

5. The play will open on March 8 ~~?~~ .

6. This will be the best play in the history of Longwood Community Center! ✓

7. Buy tickets early to make sure you get a good seat ~~?~~ .

1. Imagine that it was your job to review the community center's play. Write a declarative sentence that describes your thoughts about it.

2. Imagine that you are the director of a play. Write an imperative sentence that you might say to one of your ~~~~

   **Answers will vary.**

3. What do you think people will say when the play is over? Write an exclamatory sentence on the line.

**37**

---

The **subject** of a sentence is what a sentence is about. A subject can be a single word, or it can be several words.

*You* need to wear a hat and mittens.
*Daffy Duck* first appeared in a cartoon in 1937.
*Toddy, Jenny, Sonia,* and *Lisa* have been friends for years.

In a statement, the subject is found before the verb.

　　　　(subject)　　(verb)
*The cricket team won* four matches in a row.

To find the subject in a question, ask yourself *Who?* or *What?* the sentence is about. Try turning the sentence into a statement to double-check your answer.

Where is *the stadium* located?    *The stadium* is located where.

**Identify It**

Circle the subject in each sentence below.

1. (The papaya) is also called a pawpaw fruit.

2. (It) has sweet pink or yellow flesh and many small, black, peppery seeds.

3. (The skin) of a kiwi is fuzzy and brown.

4. (Mangoes) grow in tropical climates all around the world.

5. Have (you) ever heard of ugli fruit?

6. (It) is a combination of a grapefruit and a tangerine.

| Tip | A command usually begins with a verb. The subject is understood to be *you,* even if the word *you* is not in the sentence. Put the flowers in the vase.　(You) put the flowers in the vase. Leave the map in the car.　(You) leave the map in the car. |
|---|---|

**38**

---

# Answer Key

**Complete It**

Each sentence below is missing a subject. Find the subject in the box that best fits each sentence and write it on the line.

| | | |
|---|---|---|
| A breadfruit tree | Benjamin | |
| Monkeys | Lucy and Connor | The insides of coconuts |
| The peanut butter fruit | Passion fruit juice | |

1. **Lucy and Conner** worked together to make a fruit salad with five kinds of tropical fruits.

2. **Monkeys** are used to harvest coconuts in some places because they climb trees easily.

3. **The insides of coconuts** are filled with hard, white flesh and sweet "coconut water."

4. **A breadfruit tree** can produce more than 800 pieces of fruit in one season!

5. **Passion fruit juice** can be a refreshing drink on a hot summer day.

6. **Benjamin** cut open a star fruit and tasted one of the star-shaped slices.

7. **The peanut butter fruit** grows in Central and South America and tastes like peanut butter.

**Try It**

1. Write a sentence in which "understood *you*" is the subject.

2. Write a sentence [Answers will vary.] the subject.

**39**

---

A **predicate** tells what the subject of a sentence is or does. The predicate always includes the verb. Finding the verb can help you identify the predicate.

In the sentences below, the verbs are in bold. The predicates are in italics.

> Quan's grandparents **live** *in Vietnam.*
> The Johnsons **brought** *a kite to the park.*
> My aunt and uncle **have** *a rooftop garden.*

**Identify It**

In each sentence below, underline the complete predicate. Then, circle the verb.

On a sunny Saturday afternoon, Tierra and Cody (walked) to the library. They (passed) the recreation center, their school, and Burnside Park. Cody (waved) to Mr. Crockett. Every weekend, he and his dad (bought) peanuts for the ducks from Mr. Crockett.

Tierra and Cody (crossed) the street at the crosswalk. They (walked) past the large lions and up the library's wide marble stairs. Inside the building, Tierra and Cody (paused) in the cool, dim entryway. Their favorite tradition (was throwing) a few pennies into the wishing pond. Neither Tierra nor Cody (told) anyone their library wishes. They (put) away their change. Then, they (headed) toward the children's section and Mrs. Winklebaum's desk.

**40**

---

**Match It**

One box below is filled with subjects. One box is filled with predicates. Match each subject to a predicate. Then, write the complete sentences on the lines below.

| Subjects | Predicates |
|---|---|
| Mrs. Winklebaum | are members of the Bookworm Summer Reading Club. |
| The library | likes to read books about dinosaurs and ancient cities. |
| Tierra and Cody | were stacked on the librarian's desk. |
| Cody | was built in 1911. |
| Many books and papers | [Order of answers may vary.] a stamp for |

1. Mrs. Winklebaum gave Tierra and Cody a stamp for each book they read.

2. Tierra and Cody are members of the Bookworm Summer Reading Club.

3. Cody likes to read books about dinosaurs and ancient cities.

4. Many books and papers were stacked on the librarian's desk.

5. The library was built in 1911.

**Try It**

Write a short paragraph about a person or place in your community. Underline the predicate in each sentence.

[Answers will vary.]

**41**

---

A **direct object** is a noun or pronoun that receives the action of the verb. Find the direct object in a sentence by asking *Whom?* or *What?* about the verb.

> Mr. Suzuki bought *a new computer.*
>    Bought what? *a new computer*
> The police helped *the frightened woman.*
>    Helped whom? *the frightened woman*
> Alexi mailed *the package* to her sister.
>    Mailed what? *the package*

**Identify It**

Underline the verb in each sentence below. Then, circle the direct object.

1. The members of the hockey team signed (autographs) for their fans.

2. The forward shot (the puck) across the rink.

3. The referee called (a penalty).

4. The goalie quickly blocked (the puck).

5. Sam bought (a hockey jersey) with Wayne Gretzky's name on it.

6. The referee gave (a penalty shot) to a player on the other team.

7. Angela Ruggiero and Kristin King play (hockey) for the U.S. National Team.

8. The Toronto Aeros beat (the Montreal Axion) in the 2005 NWHL Championship.

**42**

## Identify It

Read each sentence below. If the underlined words are the direct object, make a check mark on the line. If they are not the direct object, make an **X** on the line. Then, find the correct direct object and circle it.

1. ✓ I saw <u>my first hockey game</u> yesterday.
2. X Uncle Gil and <u>my cousin Cristina</u> took (me.)
3. ✓ Hundreds of people filled <u>the arena</u>.
4. ✓ Uncle Gil explained <u>each play</u> to me.
5. X During the game, <u>the puck</u> hit the (dividing glass) at an incredible speed.
6. ✓ It startled <u>me</u>, and I jumped!
7. X Cristina <u>shot</u> some (photographs) of her favorite players.
8. X Cristina plays (roller hockey) <u>with some kids from her school.</u>

## Try It

Write three sentences on the lines below. Make sure each sentence has a direct object.

1. _____
2. _____ Answers will vary. _____
3. _____

**43**

---

The **subject** of a sentence is what a sentence is about.
*The highest mountain in North America* is in Denali National Park.
*Grandma Ruth* likes to garden and play tennis.

To find the subject in a question, ask yourself who or what the sentence is about. Double-check your answer by turning the sentence into a statement.
Will *Gabrielle* ride her bike or walk?
*Gabrielle* will ride her bike or walk.

In a command, the subject is "understood *you*."
Use scrap paper for the art project.
(*You*) use scrap paper for the art project.

A **predicate** tells what the subject of a sentence is or does. The predicate includes the verb.
The chestnut horse *grazes in the meadow*.
Mr. Vogel *planted a butterfly garden*.

A **direct object** is a noun or pronoun that receives the action of the verb. Find the direct object in a sentence by asking *Whom?* or *What?* about the verb.
Nathan takes *tae kwon do*.   Takes what? *tae kwon do*
Elizabeth sent *an e-mail* to Habib.   Sent what? *an e-mail*

## Putting It Together

In each sentence, underline the subject once and the predicate twice.

1. <u>Lynne Cox</u> <u><u>is a long-distance ocean swimmer</u></u>.
2. <u>She</u> <u><u>set records for swimming the Catalina Channel and the English Channel</u></u>.
3. <u>Doctors and scientists</u> <u><u>can't explain her achievements</u></u>.
4. <u><u>Can</u></u> <u>you</u> <u><u>imagine swimming in 33°F water</u></u>?

**44**

---

Read the sentences below. If the underlined phrase is the subject, write **S** on the line. If it is a predicate, write **P**. If it is a direct object, write **DO**.

1. DO Lynne Cox began <u>her open-water swims</u> as a child.
2. P As a teenager, she <u>swam California's Catalina Channel</u>.
3. DO She swam <u>21 miles</u> in about 12 hours.
4. S <u>Lynne</u> swam from Alaska to the Soviet Union in 1987.
5. P This <u>happened during the Cold War</u>.
6. S <u>America and the Soviet Union</u> did not have good relations.
7. DO Lynne's swim helped <u>the two countries</u> begin to form a bond.
8. S (You) Read more about Lynne at her Web site, www.lynnecox.org.

In each sentence below, circle the verb. Then, draw an arrow from the verb to the direct object.

1. In 2002, Lynne (swam) a mile in the waters of Antarctica.
2. She (saw) icebergs during her swim.
3. It (took) 25 minutes to complete.
4. Most people (can't survive) such cold temperatures.
5. Lynne (has trained) her body to adjust.
6. Her blood (keeps) her important organs warm.

**45**

---

A sentence is a group of words that contains a complete thought and has a subject and a predicate. A **sentence fragment** is part of a sentence, or an incomplete sentence. A sentence fragment may be a subject, a predicate, or just a few words grouped together. Sentence fragments cannot stand alone.

| Sentence Fragment: | Sentence: |
|---|---|
| *Played the piano.* | *Joe played the piano.* |
| *In the morning.* | *In the morning, Sara ran two miles.* |

## Identify It

Read each item below. If it is a complete sentence, write **C** on the line. If it is a sentence fragment, write an **F** on the line.

1. F Painted an underwater scene on the walls of the room.
2. F After Leo and Nina moved the furniture.
3. C Grandpa watered the plants.
4. C The ladybug climbed onto the leaf.
5. F Rained for four days.
6. F The boys and their teacher.
7. C The biologist peered through his microscope.
8. F Put the books in a paper bag and carried them to the car.
9. C Mom goes bowling on Tuesdays.

**46**

## Page 47

**Rewrite It**

Read the sentence fragments below. Add words to each fragment to form a complete sentence. Write the sentences on the lines. Do not forget to use capital letters and end marks where they are needed.

1. went to the movies on Saturday afternoon

2. always enjoys movies about

3. the theater was full, but some seats

4. the funniest part **Answers will vary.**

5. ordered a bucket of popcorn to share

6. I think that the best movies

**Try It**

Write three sentence fragments on a separate sheet of paper. On the lines below, write your fragments as complete sentences.

1. 
2. **Answers will vary.**
3. 

## Page 48

A **compound sentence** contains two or more complete sentences. The sentences are joined by a comma and a conjunction like *and, or,* or *but.*

The children went swimming, *and* the adults talked for hours.
We will go to the car show, *or* we will go shopping.
Raphael went to the market, *but* they were out of tomatoes.

A sentence that has two subjects or two verbs is not always a compound sentence. Remember, there must be two complete subjects and predicates to form a compound.

(subject)　(predicate)　(predicate)
<u>Simple:</u> *Sammy put on his uniform and walked down the stairs.*

(subject)　(predicate)　(subject)　(predicate)
<u>Compound:</u> *Sammy put on a hat, and he walked down the stairs.*

**Identify It**

Read the diary entry below. Underline the four compound sentences.

Dear Diary,
　　Last weekend, I visited my aunt and uncle. <u>They live in a house in the country, but it isn't a real farm.</u> <u>The only animals they have are barn cats and a sheepdog, but they do own five acres of land.</u>
　　Uncle Spencer and I decided to go exploring. We packed a lunch and headed across the big field behind his house. <u>We walked for about an hour, and I spotted several deer and a turkey.</u> Uncle Spencer and I found a great spot for lunch.
　　After lunch, we decided to poke around some more and see what we could find. My uncle found a brick with the year 1888 on it. I found the top of an old desk.
　　"I think this is an old schoolhouse!" exclaimed Uncle Spencer. <u>"Let's do some research, and we'll find our for sure."</u>

## Page 49

**Complete It**

Read each sentence below. If it is a compound sentence, make a check mark on the line. If it is not a compound sentence, make an **X** on the line. Then, add words to the sentence to turn it into a compound.

　　**^ – insert words**

Example: __X__ I looked out the window ^and I could see for miles.

1. __✓__ My u **Answers may vary. Possible answers:** ok.
　　　　　　　　**thought about**
2. __✓__ The w ^ been ^ read them.
3. __X__ I wondered whose book it had been ^and when someone had last used it.
　　　　　　　　　　　　**he**
4. __X__ I picked up the chalkboard ^and showed it to Uncle Spencer.
5. __✓__ I wished there was writing on it, but decades of weather had washed everything clean.
　　　　　　　　　　　　　　**he**
6. __X__ Uncle Spencer tripped over something ^and crouched down to see what it was.
　　　　　　　　　　　　　　**he**
7. __X__ He had discovered a rusty school bell ^and shook off the damp leaves to get a better look.
　　　　　　　　　　　　　　　　　　**I**
8. __X__ I loved the mystery of digging up a little piece of the past ^and couldn't wait to learn more about what we had found.

**Try It**

What do you think happens next to Uncle Spencer and his nephew? Write a sentence that continues the story.

**Answers will vary.**

## Page 50

**Run-on sentences** are sentences that are too long or contain too much information. Sometimes, adding a comma and a conjunction like *and, or,* or *but* will fix the run-on. Other times, the run-on sentence must be split into two separate sentences or rewritten.

In the examples that follow, the first sentence is a run-on. The next two sentences show different ways to fix a run-on sentence.

<u>Run-on:</u> Darcy speaks Spanish her friend Logan speaks French.
　　　　Darcy speaks Spanish, *and* her friend Logan speaks French.
　　　　Darcy speaks Spanish. Her friend Logan speaks French.

**Identify It**

Read each sentence below. If it is a complete sentence, make a check mark on the line. If it is a run-on sentence, write **RO** on the line. Then, make a slash (/) where you would divide the sentence.

1. __✓__ Wolves don't have a very good reputation.

2. __✓__ Do you remember the story of Little Red Riding Hood or the Three Little Pigs?

3. __RO__ Some people are frightened by these wild creatures/they believe that wolves attack easily.

4. __RO__ Wolves are shy around humans/they would prefer not to be seen.

5. __✓__ In the American West, wolves hunt animals like deer and rabbits.

6. __RO__ They can be a problem for farmers/they sometimes attack sheep or cattle.

7. __RO__ A wolf's coat is thick and beautiful/it is made of two layers of fur.

8. __RO__ The top layer keeps away water and dirt/the bottom layer keeps the animal warm.

**Proof It**

Read the run-on sentences below. Correct each sentence using proofreading marks. You may need to add a comma and a conjunction, or you may need to divide it into two sentences. If you make two separate sentences, remember to capitalize the first word of the new sentence.

> ^ – inserts words and punctuation
> ≡ – capitalizes a letter

1. Wolves are related to dogs their paws, legs, and jaws are stronger.

2. Wolves live and travel in packs there are usually between two and six wolves in a pack.

3. A pack is usually led by a male and a female they are the alpha wolves.

**Answers will vary.**

4. Alpha wolves have the highest rank in a pack they have the most freedom.

5. Wolves in the wild live six to nine years they can live about twice as long in captivity.

6. People who visit Yellowstone Park often see wolves the wolves don't usually come too close.

**Try It**

Write two run-on sentences on a separate sheet of paper about an animal that you find interesting. On the lines below, correct your run-on sentences.

1. _____

2. _____

**Answers will vary.**

**51**

---

A **sentence fragment** is part of a sentence, or an incomplete sentence. Sentence fragments cannot stand alone.
> Sentence Fragment: *During the show*
> Sentence: *During the show, Joe played the piano.*

A **compound sentence** contains two or more complete sentences. The sentences are joined by a comma and a conjunction like *and, or,* or *but.*
> Shannon made a collage**,** *and* Kahlil drew a picture.

**Run-on sentences** are sentences that are too long or contain too much information. Adding a comma and a conjunction can make a compound sentence. It can also be split into two separate, complete sentences.

Bamboo is the fastest growing plant some species can grow about

a foot in a day. Most bamboo grows in East and Southeast Asia it

also grows in other tropical climates.

**Putting It Together**

Read each item below. If it is a fragment, write **F** on the line. If it is a run-on sentence, write **RO** on the line. If it is a compound sentence, write **C** on the line.

1. _RO_ The word *piano* comes from the Italian word *pianoforte* it means *soft-loud.*

2. _C_ Bartolomeo Cristofori invented the piano, but no one is sure of the exact date.

3. _F_ Two of his pianos, from the 1720s.

4. _F_ Similar to the clavichord and harpsichord.

5. _C_ The keys move felt-covered hammers, and the hammers cause the strings to vibrate and create sound.

**52**

---

Read the paragraph below. Underline the three compound sentences. Then, find the three run-on sentences. Use proofreading marks to correct them.

> ^ – inserts words and punctuation
> ≡ – capitalizes a letter

A modern piano has 88 keys it covers a range of more than seven octaves. Some older **Answers will vary.** ave an extra set of keys they are hidden under a small lid. Today, there are two main types of pianos. The grand piano is about six to nine feet long, and it sounds best when played in a room with high ceilings. Concert grand pianos are usually used for public shows because longer pianos often have better sound. Upright pianos have vertical strings, and grand pianos have horizontal strings. Vertical pianos don't take up as much space grand pianos are more sensitive to the player's touch.

Add words to each sentence fragment to form a complete sentence. Write the sentences on the lines. Do not forget to use capital letters and end marks where they are needed.

1. plays the piano

2. takes lessons once a week

**Answers will vary.**

3. the teacher, Mr. Valentine,

**53**

---

**Combining sentences** can help a writer avoid repeating words. It can also make the writing read more smoothly. If two sentences tell about the same thing, they can be combined. If the subject of the sentence changes from singular to plural (or vice-versa), remember to change the verb so that it agrees.

> Combining Subjects:
> *Olivia* lives on 42nd Street. *Natalie* lives on 42nd Street.
> *Olivia and Natalie* live on 42nd Street.

> Combining Direct Objects:
> Takumi ate *a turkey sandwich.* Takumi ate *a crisp, green apple.*
> Takumi ate *a turkey sandwich and a crisp, green apple.*

**Identify It**

Read each set of sentences below. If the sentences can be combined, make a check mark on the line. If they tell about different things and cannot be combined, make an **X** on the line.

1. _✓_ The Big Dipper is a well-known constellation. Orion is a well-known constellation.

2. _✓_ Alisha used her telescope to see Aquarius. Alisha used her telescope to see Pegasus.

3. _✓_ Groups of stars may be named after animals or objects. Some are named after heroes of mythology.

4. _X_ Some constellations can be seen only from the Northern Hemisphere. Other constellations can be seen only from the Southern Hemisphere.

5. _X_ You can see Andromeda in the winter sky. You can see Cygnus, the swan, in the summer and fall.

**54**

**Rewrite It**

Combine each pair of sentences below into one sentence. Write the new sentence on the line.

1. Jasmine used the telescope at the observatory. Aaron used the telescope at the observatory.

   _____

2. Aaron knows a lot about stars. Jasmine is knowledgeable about stars, too.

   _____

3. In Greek mythology, Cassiopeia was a queen. In Greek mythology, Cassiopeia was Andromeda's mother.

   Answers will vary.

4. Cassiopeia can be seen all year in the Northern Hemisphere. Ursa Major and Ursa Minor can be seen all year, too.

   _____

5. Scorpius and Orion are enemies. Scorpius and Orion are visible in different seasons.

   _____

6. You can learn more about constellations online. You can also learn more about constellations in books of Greek mythology.

   _____

**55**

---

When two or more sentences tell about the same thing, they can sometimes be combined using the words *and* or *or*. If you list several things in a row, remember to place a comma after each one.

> Ryan might go for a bike ride. He might play soccer. He might go to a movie.
> Ryan might go for a bike ride, play soccer, *or* go to a movie.

**Complete It**

Read the sentences below. Fill in each blank with a comma or the missing word or words.

1. Isabel looked at the recipes in her cookbook. She checked the cupboards for ingredients.

   Isabel _____**looked**_____ at the recipes in her cookbook and _____**checked**_____ the cupboards for ingredients.

2. Isabel and Simon might make oatmeal-banana bread. They might bake oatmeal-raisin cookies.

   **Isabel and Simon** might make oatmeal-banana bread**,** or _____**they**_____ might bake oatmeal-raisin cookies.

3. Isabel likes raisins better than bananas. She decided to make oatmeal-raisin cookies.

   Isabel _____**likes**_____ raisins better than bananas and _____**decided**_____ to make oatmeal-raisin cookies.

4. Isabel and Simon measured the sugar. They added some vanilla. They cracked the eggs.

   Isabel and Simon measured the sugar**,** added some vanilla**,** _____**and**_____ cracked the eggs.

**56**

---

**Rewrite It**

Combine each set of sentences below into one sentence. Write the new sentence on the line.

1. Isabel plugged in the mixer. She beat the sugar, butter, eggs, and vanilla.

   **Isabel plugged in the mixer and beat the sugar, butter, eggs, and vanilla.**

2. Simon added the flour. He poured in the oats. He blended the ingredients.

   **Simon added the flour, poured in the oats, and blended the ingredients.**

3. Simon sprinkled raisins on top of the mixture. Simon stirred the dough.

   **Simon sprinkled raisins on top of the mixture and stirred the dough.**

4. Isabel and Simon scooped up spoonfuls of cookie dough. They dropped them onto the cookie sheet.

   **Isabel and Simon scooped up spoonfuls of cookie dough and dropped them onto the cookie sheet.**

5. The two friends cleaned up the kitchen. The two friends waited for the cookies to bake.

   **The two friends cleaned up the kitchen and waited for the cookies to bake.**

6. They might bring the cookies to school. They might save them for a picnic on Saturday.

   **They might bring the cookies to school or save them for a picnic on Saturday.**

7. Isabel's mom heard the kitchen timer ring. Isabel's mom took the cookies out of the oven.

   **Isabel's mom heard the kitchen timer ring and took the cookies out of the oven.**

**57**

---

Sentences that use adjectives to describe the same thing can often be combined. In the sentences that follow, the adjectives *blue*, *heavy*, and *rectangular* all describe *box*. Remember to use commas after each item in a series, except the last.

> Liam carried the *blue* box up the stairs. The box was *rectangular* and heavy.
> Liam carried the *heavy*, *rectangular*, *blue* box up the stairs.

> The spelling bee contestants were *young*. They felt *excited*. They were also *nervous*.
> The *young* spelling bee contestants were *excited* and *nervous*.

**Identify It**

There are three pairs of sentences that can be combined in the paragraphs below. Underline each pair.

The Metropolitan Museum of Art is a large museum. It is an important museum. Many people call it "The Met." It is located near Central Park in New York City. The collection of artworks is valuable. It is impressive. There are nearly three million objects housed at the museum. It would take about five and a half years to look at everything if you spent one minute per object.

Some displays and events are just for children. If you have a chance to visit the museum, you should be sure to see the Egyptian Temple of Dendur. The temple was brought to America from Egypt by ship. The temple is more than 2,000 years old. The temple is very popular with tourists.

**58**

---

**Rewrite It**

Combine each set of sentences below into a single sentence. Write the new sentence on the line.

1. The enormous painting hanging in the hall was bright. It was colorful.

2. Vicente touched the stone sculpture of a bird. It felt smooth. It felt cold.

3. The collage mad[e] ~~~ nteresting. The collage was unu ~~~

   *Answers will vary.*

4. The print hanging in the gallery was made with vegetable dyes. The print was beautiful.

5. The ancient carving was tiny and intricate. It was wooden.

**Try It**

1. Write two sentences that describe an object you might see in a museum. Use a different adjective in each sentence.

   *Answers will vary.*

2. Now, write a sentence that combines the two sentences you wrote.

**59**

---

**Putting It Together**

Combine each set of sentences below into a single sentence. Write the new sentence on the line.

1. The Amazon rain forest is located in South America. It is the largest rain forest in the world.

   **The Amazon rain forest is located in South America and is the largest rain forest in the world.**

2. Tropical rain forests are hot. They are moist. Rain forests are lush.

   **Tropical rain forests are hot, moist, and lush.**

3. Some species of insects are unique to the rain forests. Some animals are unique to the rain forests.

   **Some species of insects and animals are unique to the rain forests.**

4. Most rain forest insects live high in the canopy. Most rain forest insects are beetles.

   **Most rain forest insects are beetles and live high in the canopy.**

There are three pairs of sentences that can be combined in the paragraphs below. Underline each pair.

The animals of the rain forest interest scientists. The animals of the rain forest are fascinating. Scientists have identified some species but know little about them. Other species have yet to be discovered.

In the space of only a few miles, more than 100 types of mammals can be found. Some rain forest animals live on the ground. Many spend a good deal of time in the canopy. The canopy is high above the forest floor. The plants and animals in a rain forest often depend on each other. They may use one another for food, protection, shelter, and pollination.

**61**

---

Capitalize the **names of specific people and pets**.

    Sally named the kittens Claudia, Clemson, Carter, and Camille.
    Jane Goodall studies chimpanzees.

A **title** gives more information about who a person is. **Titles that come before a name** and **titles of respect** are capitalized.

| | | |
|---|---|---|
| Grandma Pearl | Uncle Santos | Mayor Devlin |
| Officer Bernhardt | Nurse Capshaw | Judge May Bennett |
| Ms. Choudhry | Dr. Rozic | Mr. Zhu |

If a title is not used with a name, it is not capitalized.

    My *grandpa* collects Civil War uniforms.
    The *nurse* gave me a bandage.

But if a title is used as a name, it is capitalized.

    On Sunday, Grandpa made scrambled eggs.
    Will Mom pick us up today?

**Complete It**

Read the sentences below. Underline the word in parentheses that correctly completes each sentence and write it on the line.

1. On Friday afternoon, I have an appointment with __Dr.__ Ali. (dr., <u>Dr.</u>)

2. My __aunt__ lives in an apartment above a pet store. (Aunt, <u>aunt</u>)

3. Ana is going to interview her grandpa, who was a __judge__ for 42 years. (Judge, <u>judge</u>)

4. Our neighbors got a chinchilla and named it __Harriet__. (harriet, <u>Harriet</u>)

5. Which game did you and your __dad__ play? (<u>dad</u>, Dad)

6. Lindsay's uncle is __Captain__ O'Hara. (<u>Captain</u>, captain)

**62**

---

**Proof It**

Read the diary entry below. Use proofreading marks to correct the 11 mistakes in capitalization.

≡ - capitalize a letter
/ - lowercase a letter

Dear Diary,

    I have been researching my family tree. I have learned many interesting things about my relatives. For example, grandma Helen was a trapeze artist. She did a show with an elephant named farley. Mom also told me that uncle thomas was a famous author in the early 1900s. He wrote more than 20 books. I even found out that I am a distant cousin of president Hoover!

    Mayor Glass is the Mayor of the town where mom's family lived. I have e-mailed her for information from the town's records. I want to learn about a woman named rose amelia saxon. I was named after her, but I don't know anything about her life.

**Try It**

1. Write the names of three people you know who have titles before their names.

   *Answers will vary.*

2. Think of two peo[ple] ~~~ e their names below.

   Person:_____    Pet:_____

   Person:_____    Pet:_____

**63**

---

---

The **names of specific places** always begin with a capital letter.

Appalachian Mountains    Baltimore, Maryland
India    Colgate University
Lakewood Little Theater    Portland Art Museum

**Complete It**
Answer each question below using a complete sentence. Remember to capitalize the names of specific places.

1. What school do you attend?
   _____

2. If you could visit any country in the world, where would you go?
   _____

3. In what city and state do you live? _____

   _____ Answers will vary. _____

4. Which planet would you most like to visit? Why?
   _____

5. Name a museum, zoo, park, or library you have visited.
   _____

**Tip**
• The names of the planets begin with a capital letter.
• When *Earth* refers to the planet, capitalize it. When it refers to the soil or ground, lowercase it.
   The third planet from the sun is *Earth*.
   The *earth* in this area is rich with nutrients.

**64**

---

**Proof It**
Read the brochure below. There are 21 mistakes in capitalization. Use proofreading marks to correct the errors.

= - capitalize a letter
/ - lowercase a letter

Example: The wettest place in the United States is mount waialeale in the State of Hawaii.

Welcome to Miami, florida, where the sun is always shining!

We are glad you have decided to make our beautiful city your home!
We are located on the Miami river, between the Everglades and the atlantic Ocean.
We are a diverse city with many citizens from Latin America, the Caribbean, and Europe.

Once you are settled in your new home, it will be time to do some exploring. The following attractions are fun for all newcomers—old and young alike.
• Coconut Grove
• the Miami art museum
• the Miami seaquarium
• Parrot Jungle Island
• Little Havana
• the fairchild Tropical Gardens

Also be sure to visit the Miami-Dade public library on west Flagler Street, Bicentennial park on Biscayne Boulevard, and the farmers' market at the corner of Miami Avenue and Flagler street.

**Try It**
Imagine that someone has just moved to your hometown from another state. Write a short paragraph telling them about some places they could visit. Use at least four specific place names in your paragraph.

_____ Answers will vary. _____

**65**

---

The **days of the week** each begin with a capital letter.
   Sunday, Monday, Tuesday, Wednesday, Thursday, Friday, Saturday

The **months** of the year are capitalized.
   January, February, March, April, May, June, July,
   August, September, October, November, December

The **names of holidays** are capitalized.
   Earth Day    Father's Day    New Year's Eve    Memorial Day

**Complete It**
Fill in the blanks below with the words in parentheses. Use capital letters when needed.

1. Theodore's favorite holiday is __Thanksgiving__. (thanksgiving)

2. Veronica prefers __Valentine's Day__. (valentine's day)

3. Felix and Franny were both born on an icy ___Friday___ in __February__. (friday/february)

4. ___August___ is a very busy month for Andre and Angelina. (august)

5. On __Veteran's Day__, Mr. Victor Vega has a reunion with soldiers from his platoon. (veteran's day)

6. In __September__, Sanjana will travel to Syria, Singapore, Sweden, and Sicily. (september)

7. Maureen meets Morgan for lunch every __Monday__. (monday)

8. Greg will travel to Punxsutawney, Pennsylvania for __Groundhog's Day__. (groundhog's day)

**66**

---

**Rewrite It**
Rewrite each sentence below using capital letters for dates and holidays.

1. mother's day always falls on the second sunday in may.

   Mother's Day always falls on the second Sunday in May.

2. China and Vietnam do not celebrate new year's day on january 1.

   China and Vietnam do not celebrate New Year's Day on January 1.

3. rosh hashanah and yom kippur are Jewish holidays celebrated in september.

   Rosh Hashanah and Yom Kippur are Jewish holidays celebrated in September.

4. The fourth thursday in november is thanksgiving.

   The fourth Thursday in November is Thanksgiving.

5. kwanzaa is a holiday that begins on december 26 and celebrates the goodness of life.

   Kwanzaa is a holiday that begins on December 26 and celebrates the goodness of life.

6. independence day has been celebrated on july 4 since 1777.

   Independence Day has been celebrated on July 4 since 1777.

**Try It**
1. Write the month and year you were born on the line below.

2. Write the name ___ Answers will vary. ___ ur birthday.

**67**

## Page 68

The **titles of books, movies, and songs** are capitalized. Do not capitalize prepositions, articles, or conjunctions, like *of, the, and, in, to, a, an,* and *from,* unless they are the first or last word of a title.

**Books**
Because of Winn-Dixie
Tuck Everlasting
A Long Way from Chicago

**Movies**
The Incredibles
The Polar Express
Harriet the Spy

**Songs**
"Here Comes the Sun"
"Getting to Know You"
"At the Bottom of the Sea"

**Complete It**
Fill the blanks below with the titles of books, movies, or songs. Use capital letters where they are needed. Remember to underline book and movie titles. Use quotation marks with song titles.

1. The last book I read was

2. If I were a movie critic, I would *not* give a "thumbs-up" to

3. One of my favorite songs when I was little was

4. I would re ____ **Answers will vary.**

5. I know all the words to the song

6. The best movie I've seen this year is

7. I like the book ____ because the characters seem like real people.

8. I laughed incredibly hard when I saw the movie

## Page 69

**Proof It**
Read the letter below. There are 14 mistakes in capitalization. Use proofreading marks to correct the mistakes.

☰ – capitalize a letter
/ – lowercase a letter

*February 23*

Dear Kyle,

How's life in Texas? It's time for our monthly book and movie review. I read *Tales/1/. Fourth Grade* nothing last week, and I thought it was hilarious. The main character has a pesky younger brother, so I know you could relate to it. *dolphin treasure* by Wayne Grover is a great adventure. If you are in the mood for a mystery, I would highly recommend the *Canoe Trip mystery.*

I finally saw the movie *holes.* It is as good as the book, and I guarantee that you will not be disappointed. When you have a chance, you should also see *spy kids* and *Robots.*

It's time for me to wrap this up. I have a big pile of homework to do. Serena has been listening to our parents' oldies CD all afternoon. I am really tired of hearing "Splish Splash," "rockin' robin," and "lollipop"!

Your favorite cousin,

Micah

**Try It**
Imagine that you published a book, wrote a song, and directed a movie. What would you name your creations? Write the titles on the lines below.

**Answers will vary.**

## Page 70

Capitalize the names of **specific people and pets**.
 My sister, **N**ikki, wrote a story about a pet monkey named **S**quizzle.
Capitalize **titles that come before a name**.
 **A**unt Linh  **S**enator Rivera  **M**rs. Wasserbauer  **D**r. Oakley
Do not capitalize titles that are used alone, unless they are used as a name.
 My *dad* plays basketball.   I asked *Dad* to close the windows.
Capitalize the **names of specific places**.
 **L**inden **H**ospital  **Q**uincy, **M**assachusetts  **G**rady **P**reschool  **B**razil
The **days of the week** and **months of the year** begin with a capital letter.
 **T**uesday, **F**riday, **S**unday   **A**pril, **J**une, **O**ctober, **D**ecember
The names of holidays are capitalized.
 **P**resident's **D**ay  **I**ndependence **D**ay  **M**other's **D**ay
The **titles of books, movies, and songs** are capitalized. Do not capitalize prepositions, articles, or conjunctions unless they are the first or last word of a title.
 Barbara Park wrote **T**he **K**id in the **R**ed **J**acket.

**Putting It Together**
Complete each sentence below with the words in parentheses. Some of the words will need to be capitalized, and others will not.

1. My ___**grandpa**___ (grandpa) and his dog, ___**Callie**___ (callie), are coming to see our new house.

2. They are coming on ___**Friday**___ (friday) morning and staying through ___**Labor Day**___ (labor day).

3. I gave ___**Grandpa**___ (grandpa) directions from his office on **Wellspring Street** (wellspring street).

4. "Our house is a mile past ___**Dr. Twombly's**___ (dr. twombly's) office on ___**Carter Avenue**___ (carter avenue)," I said.

## Page 71

There are 17 mistakes in capitalization in the datebook entries below. Correct the mistakes using proofreading marks.

☰ – capitalize a letter
/ – lowercase a letter

**Dates to Remember**

February 14 – **V**alentine's **D**ay party
March 3 – Take Milo and **R**oxy to the vet at 3:30
March 8 – **U**ncle Tommy's flight from **C**hile arrives at 6:30
March 12 – Birthday party for Katie Wang—1426 East **w**illow drive
March 19 – Order The Wind **i**n **t**he Willows and **C**harlotte's **W**eb for **B**righton School book drive
March 30 – Hailey's appointment with **D**r. Traynor at 4:15
April 9 – Free tickets at **C**lover Children's Museum, **F**riday-Sunday

Rewrite the sentences below using capital letters where needed.

1. beverly cleary wrote ralph s. mouse and ramona and her mother.
**Beverly Cleary wrote Ralph S. Mouse, Ramona and Her Mother.**

2. officer gomez lives and works in santa ana, california.
**Officer Gomez lives and works in Santa Ana, California.**

3. on father's day, we rented the movies hook and a bug's life.
**On Father's Day, we rented the movies Hook and A Bug's Life.**

4. julie andrews sang "spoonful of sugar" in the movie mary poppins.
**Julie Andrews sang "Spoonful of Sugar" in the movie Mary Poppins.**

A **period** is an end mark that follows a statement or a command. Use a period to end a declarative or an imperative sentence.

    Washington borders Oregon and Idaho.   Put the marbles in the jar.

Periods also follow **abbreviations**. Use a period after an **initial**, or letter that stands for a name.

    E. B. White        George W. Bush        Danielle A. Williams

**People's titles** are usually abbreviated when they come before a name.

    Mrs. = Mistress        Mr. = Mister        Dr. = Doctor

The **days of the week** and the **months of the year** are often abbreviated.

    Fri. afternoon    Oct. 28, 1988    Mon.–Thurs.    Jan. 15

**Types of streets** are abbreviated in addresses.

    Caroline Blvd.        Rockingham Rd.        Huckleberry Ave.

**Measurements** can also be abbreviated.

    in. = inch    ft. = feet    yd. = yard    mi. = mile    oz. = ounce
    pt. = pint    qt. = quart    gal. = gallon    lb. = pound    c. = cup

**Rewrite It**

Read each sentence below. Then, rewrite the bold words using an abbreviation.

1. Robbie is 4 **feet** _ft._ 11 **inches** _in._ tall.

2. The Hughes family is moving to Redwing **Court** _Ct._.

3. Mom bought a **pint** _pt._ of blueberries and a **quart** _qt._ of strawberries.

4. Vikram's birthday is **Thursday** _Thurs._, **August** _Aug._ 8.

5. **Alan Alexander** _A.A._ Milne is the author of the Winnie the Pooh books.

**72**

---

**Proof It**

Read the brochure below. It is missing 18 periods. Add the periods where they are needed. Remember to circle them so that they are easy to see.

### Time to take a dip at Valley Ridge Pool!

Valley Ridge Pool will be open for the summer from Mon., May 30–Sat., Sept.. Join us for swimming lessons, lap swim, water aerobics, and synchronized swimming. Our low dive is 4 ft. tall. The high dive is 16 ft. tall. We have a snack bar, a kiddie pool, showers, and a 30-yd. pool. Children under 3 ft. tall must be accompanied by an adult.

Pool Manager: Mr. J.P. Stevens
Lifeguards: Cassidy L. Wickline, Grace Yamamoto, P. Ellis Snyder
Pool Hours: Mon.–Sat.: 9 a.m. until 7 p.m. Sun.: noon until 6 p.m.
Location: the corner of Cherry Ln. and Bellhaven St.

**Try It**

Interview a friend. Write your friend's answers on the lines below using abbreviations as often as possible.

What is your complete name? _____

What is your address? _____

How tall are you? _____ | Answers will vary. |

When is your birthday? _____

**73**

---

Use a **question mark** to end a sentence that asks a question.

    Did you put away the milk**?**
    What type of currency do people use in Japan**?**

Use an **exclamation point** to end a sentence that expresses strong feelings, like excitement, happiness, surprise, anger, and fear.

    Don't take that bicycle**!**        My computer crashed**!**

**Complete It**

Read the interview below. Some sentences are missing end marks. Complete the sentences with a question mark or an exclamation point.

**Mateo:** How did you first become interested in reptiles?

**Mr. O'Toole:** I've been interested since I was a small boy. I caught my first lizard when I was only two **!**

**Mateo:** Where have your travels taken you **?**

**Mr. O'Toole:** I've visited many fascinating countries, like Brazil, Thailand, and Australia. I have traveled all the way around the world three times!

**Mateo:** Wow **!** That's incredible **!**

**Mr. O'Toole:** Are you interested in traveling, Mateo **?**

**Mateo:** Yes, I'd love to see the world one day. Which expedition was your favorite **?**

**Mr. O'Toole:** Borneo is at the top of my list. I had some interesting experiences with unusual reptiles there.

**Mateo:** Did you ever feel like you were in serious danger **?**

**Mr. O'Toole:** More times than I can count **!** It's just part of the job.

**74**

---

**Proof It**

There are seven mistakes in punctuation in the paragraphs below. Delete incorrect end marks and add question marks or exclamation points where they are needed.

| ⌐ - deletes punctuation |
| ^ - inserts punctuation |

    Reptiles are cold-blooded animals that are covered with scales. Most reptiles hatch from eggs. Unlike amphibians, their scaly skin is not moist. It also does not let water in. There are more than 7,000 species of reptiles in the world today. How many of them are you familiar with?

    Turtles are interesting creatures. A turtle's shell is a portable type of protection. The smallest turtles are only about four inches long. The largest can weigh about 2,000 pounds. Turtles also have an amazing life span. Giant tortoises can live to be 150 years old.

    Have you ever heard of tuataras? Tuataras are similar to lizards. Scientists sometimes call them "living fossils." Can you guess why? This type of reptile is older than the dinosaurs. Scientists believe that tuataras may have existed for more than 225 million years. The only place they are still found today is on some islands near New Zealand.

**Try It**

On the lines below, continue the interview from page 74. End one sentence with a question mark and one with an exclamation point.

Mateo: _____

Mr. O'Toole: _____ Answers will vary. _____

**75**

A **period** follows a statement or a command.
Elizabeth Cady Stanton fought for voting rights.
Give me the peanuts, please.

A period is used after **initials** and after people's titles.
Franklin D. Roosevelt    T. S. Eliot    Mrs. Bell    Dr. Kovitch

The **days of the week**, **months of the year**, and **types of streets** are often abbreviated.
Wed. morning        Dec. 4, 2004        Maple Ave.

**Measurements** are often abbreviated.
in. = inch    ft. = feet    yd. = yard    mi. = mile    oz. = ounce
pt. = pint    qt. = quart    gal. = gallon    lb. = pound    c. = cup

A **question mark** ends a question.
Is Selma your cousin?
Did you know that a group of toads is called a *knot*?

An **exclamation point** ends a sentence that expresses strong feeling.
I forgot my homework!    Congratulations on your graduation!

**Putting It Together**
Read each item below. Write the letter of the correct abbreviation in the space.

1. __a__ 25 pounds          **a.** 25 lbs.          **b.** 25 poun.
2. __a__ Robin Hood Drive    **a.** Robin Hood Dr.    **b.** Robin Hood Drv.
3. __b__ Elwyn Brooks White  **a.** EB. White        **b.** E. B. White
4. __a__ Monday–Friday       **a.** Mon.–Fri.        **b.** Mo.–Fr.
5. __b__ 8-ounce glass        **a.** 8-oun. glass      **b.** 8-oz. glass
6. __a__ January 1, 2000      **a.** Jan. 1, 2000      **b.** Jnry. 1, 2000

76

---

Read the postcard that follows. Insert the correct punctuation marks in the spaces. You will use three periods, two question marks, and two exclamation points.

Aug. 18, 2007

Dear Chloe,

How are you? I am writing from Calaveras Big Trees State Park in California. I think you would really like to visit this park. It's hard to describe how amazing the redwood trees are. The largest tree here is the Louis Agassiz tree. It is about 250 feet tall! Experts believe these trees could continue growing forever. The oldest sequoia redwood is believed to be 3,300 years old! Can you imagine living through so much history?

We'll be heading home tomorrow. Even though the trip will be long, I'm looking forward to stopping at some interesting places along the way. See you soon!

Your friend,

Noah

Read each sentence below. If the end mark is used correctly, make a check mark on the line. If you find an error, make an **X** on the line. Use proofreading marks to correct the mistakes you find.

| ℯ – deletes punctuation |
| ^ – inserts punctuation |

1. __X__ There are 129 campsites at Calaveras Big Trees State Park.
2. __X__ Look how tall that tree is!
3. __✓__ General Sherman, General Grant, and Empire State are the names of trees in the park.
4. __X__ What city is located closest to the park?
5. __X__ Redwoods can grow as much as eight feet in one season!

77

---

**Commas** are used in **dates** in between the day of the month and the year. If the date is in the middle of a sentence, use a comma after the year, too.
June 20, 1973        August 11, 2001        January 1, 2006
Maria was born on April 5, 1999, when Bryce was a year old.

**Commas** are used in between the names of **cities and states** or **cities and countries**. When used in the middle of a sentence, put a comma after the name of the state or country, too.
Chicago, Illinois        Austin, Texas        Stockholm, Sweden
My family moved from Phoenix, Arizona, to San Diego, California.

**Rewrite It**
Rewrite the sentences below. Add commas where they are needed.

1. On November 7 1885 the Canadian Pacific Railway was completed.

   On November 7, 1885, the Canadian Pacific Railway was completed.

2. The railway runs from Montreal Quebec to Vancouver British Columbia.

   The railway runs from Montreal, Quebec, to Vancouver, British Columbia.

3. It also has branches in U.S. cities, like Minneapolis Minnesota and Chicago Illinois.

   It also has branches in U.S. cities, like Minneapolis, Minnesota, and Chicago, Illinois.

| Tip | Do not use a comma between a month and a year if a date is not used.
Lea went to Spain in March 1999. |

78

---

**Proof It**
Read the sentences below. Delete commas that are not used correctly. Use proofreading marks to add commas where they are needed.

| ℯ – deletes punctuation |
| ^ – inserts punctuation |

1. The last spike in the railway was driven at Craigellachie, British Columbia.
2. The first transcontinental train arrived on July 4, 1886.
3. An early part of the railway connected Winnipeg, Manitoba, with St. Paul, Minnesota.
4. The Crowsnest Pass ran from Lethbridge, Alberta, to Kootenay Lake.
5. King George VI and Queen Elizabeth traveled on the Canadian Pacific Railway in May, 1939.
6. On April 24, 1955, a new luxury passenger train, *The Canadian*, began service.
7. For about 35 years, "school cars" helped teachers reach students by train in remote areas of Ontario, Canada.

**Try It**
1. If you were traveling across the country, which two cities would you be sure to visit? Write a complete sentence to answer the question. Include the names of the cities and the states.

2. Choose a fam[ ___ Answers will vary. ___ ]hen and where he or she was born. [ ___ ] a complete sentence using the information you found.

79

---

# Answer Key

---

An **introductory word** is a word that begins a sentence and introduces it to the reader. When the following words appear at the beginning of a sentence, a comma should follow: *first, last, then, next, finally, however, yes, no,* and *well.*

> *Finally,* Roman gathered his books and headed out the door.
> *However,* no one had told the boys about the clubhouse.

A **series** is a list of words. Use a comma after each word in a series except the last word.

> *Jupiter, Saturn,* and *Uranus* are the three largest planets.
> Isaac packed his *books, CDs, model airplane,* and *clothes.*

When you address a person by name, a comma separates the name from the rest of the sentence. Use a comma only with **direct address**, or when you are writing or speaking directly to a person.

> *Laura,* did you hear the news?    Thanks for your advice, *Mr. Wen.*

**Proof It**
The sentences below are missing a total of eight commas. Use proofreading marks to add commas where they are needed.

| ↑ - inserts comma |
|---|

1. Jess, do you know how to make an omelet?

2. First, you must carefully crack four eggs into a bowl.

3. Then, stir in a little milk.

4. Chop up some peppers, zucchini, spinach, and cheese.

5. Finally, add all the ingredients to the skillet, and let them cook over a medium heat.

6. You give excellent instructions, Jess!

**80**

---

**Rewrite It**
Read the sentences below. Some sentences are missing commas. In others, the commas are in the wrong places. Rewrite each sentence using commas only where they are needed.

1. Aunt Kat will you help me plan a surprise party for, Mom?

   Aunt Kat, will you help me plan a surprise party for Mom?

2. First we will need to buy invitations flowers balloons and a cake.

   First, we will need to buy invitations, flowers, balloons, and a cake.

3. Mom likes strawberries whipped cream, and chocolate cake.

   Mom likes strawberries, whipped cream, and chocolate cake.

4. However we have to remember that she is allergic to nuts.

   However, we have to remember that she is allergic to nuts.

5. Can you mail the invitations by tomorrow afternoon Uncle, Tony?

   Can you mail the invitations by tomorrow afternoon, Uncle Tony?

**Try It**
1. Imagine that you were planning a surprise party for a friend or a family member. Using a complete sentence, list four people you would invite.

2. Write three sent[ Answers will vary. ]lan the party. Begin them with the words *first, next,* and *last.*

**81**

---

A **compound sentence** is made of two or more complete, simple sentences. The conjunction *and, or, but,* or *so* and a comma join the simple sentences.

> Would you like to go out for lunch, *or* have you already eaten?
> I loved the book, *but* I thought the movie was dull.
> Wisconsin is the Badger State, Minnesota is the Gopher State, *and* Oregon is the Beaver State.

**Identify It**
Read each sentence below. If it is a simple sentence, write **S** on the line. If it is a compound sentence, write **C** on the line. Then, underline each simple sentence in the compound sentence.

1. __S__ From 1849 to 1869, thousands of Americans traveled west on the Oregon Trail.

2. __C__ The trail stretched more than 2,000 miles, and it passed through what would become six states in the American West.

3. __C__ Some people traveled west to find a better life, but others were hoping to find adventure and riches.

4. __S__ The first large wagon train left from Missouri and carried more than 100 people.

5. __C__ Some pioneers made it all the way to Oregon City, but others chose to settle at different places along the trail.

6. __S__ When the first transcontinental railroad was finished in 1869, the trail was used less often.

7. __C__ Would you have been willing to make the five-month-long trip, or would you have preferred the safety of home?

**82**

---

**Proof It**
Read the paragraphs below. There are five missing commas. Add commas to the compound sentences.

| ↑ - inserts comma |
|---|

On the Oregon Trail, pioneers often used rocks as landmarks. The rocks showed the travelers how far they had come, and they reassured people that they hadn't strayed off course. Chimney Rock in western Nebraska is easy to spot. The peak soars more than 300 feet into the sky, and it can be seen from miles away. Some travelers wrote about the rock in their journals, and others made sketches of it.

Another well-known landmark is Register Cliff in Guernsey, Wyoming. Some pioneers traveling the Oregon Trail just carved their names, but others chose to leave messages in the soft limestone rock for people who came after them. The carvings marked the great distance a person had traveled, so they were a sign of pride and accomplishment. Today, the carvings give visitors a glimpse of history.

**Try It**
Imagine that you were traveling on the Oregon Trail with your family. On the lines below, write two compound sentences that describe your experiences.

| Answers will vary. |
|---|

**83**

---

## Page 85

**Putting It Together**

The letter below is missing 15 commas. Add commas where they are needed.

> ◇ – inserts comma

March 16, 2008

Dear Amit,

    My family and I decided to go to Montpelier, Vermont, to visit my grandpa during Spring Break. He makes his own maple syrup, and he promised to show us how.

    The sap began to flow a couple of weeks ago, so Grandpa tapped his trees. He used to use tin pails to collect the sap, but today he has rubber hoses that do the job. First, grandpa boiled the sap until it was sweet and thick. Next, he strained it. Finally, he poured it into glass bottles. Amit, you have never tasted anything so delicious! We have used Grandpa's syrup on pancakes, waffles, French toast, and ice cream.

    We will be back in Lexington, Kentucky, by the end of the week. I will bring you a bottle of Grandpa's fresh maple syrup.

Your friend,

Alexandra

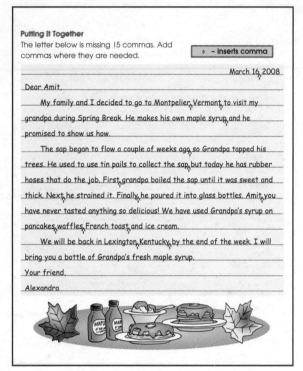

**85**

## Page 86

**Dialogue** is the exact words a person says. A set of quotation marks is used before and after dialogue.

> "Seamus goes everywhere on his skateboard."
> "This is my sister, Holly."

If the dialogue does not end the sentence, and would normally take a period, put a comma inside the quotation marks and a period at the end of the sentence.

> "Seamus goes everywhere on his skateboard," said Summer.
> "This is my sister, Holly," explained Kristen.

If the dialogue ends with a question mark or an exclamation point, place the end mark inside the quotation marks. Place a period at the end of the entire sentence.

> "Where is the Dead Sea?" asked Rob.

If part of the sentence comes before the dialogue, put a comma after that part of the sentence. Put the end mark inside the quotation marks.

> Anna exclaimed, "I can't believe the computer crashed again!"

**Complete It**

Read the sentences below. Add the correct punctuation on each line.

1. "The school fair is next weekend, isn't it?" asked Kate.

2. Munir replied, "Yes, it runs from Friday night until Sunday afternoon."

3. "I can't wait to dunk Mr. Halpern in the dunking booth!" exclaimed Ashley.

4. "We need some more volunteers to help run the booths," said Munir.

5. "Is anyone interested in helping?" he asked.

6. "Just as long as I can still run the dunking booth!" answered Ashley.

**86**

## Page 87

**Proof It**

Read the paragraphs below. Some of the quotation marks, commas, and end marks are missing or are in the wrong places. Use proofreading marks to correct the mistakes.

> ◡ – deletes punctuation
> ◇ – inserts comma
> ◡ – inserts quotations

    "I think the fair will be a great success," said Kate. "We should be able to raise a lot of money for the school library," she added.

    Munir nodded and said, "We have twice as many activities planned for this year."

    "Will there be a three-legged race and a tug-of-war?" asked Ashley.

    "I liked the beanbag toss and bobbing for apples," said Kate. "I won a goldfish and a T-shirt," she exclaimed.

    Munir smiled. "All of those activities will be a part of this year's fair," he said. "I think the best addition is the teacher's pie-eating contest. Mrs. Gabrillo and Mr. Beaumont have volunteered to bake 40 blueberry pies!"

    Kate asked, "If they bake them, they won't have to eat them, right?"

    Munir replied, "I think that was their plan!"

**Try It**

Write a short conversation between you and a teacher, relative, or friend. Place the quotation and punctuation marks in the correct places.

> Answers will vary.

**87**

## Page 88

**Titles of books, movies, and plays** are usually underlined.

> Chris Rock is the voice of Marty the Zebra in the hilarious movie <u>Madagascar</u>.
> <u>The Great Brain</u> is overdue at the library.
> Stone Theater is producing <u>The Legend of Sleepy Hollow</u>.

**Titles of songs, poems, and stories** are set in quotation marks.

> Robin, Andy, and Beatriz performed the song "Monster Mash."
> I memorized the poem "Stopping by Woods on a Snowy Evening" by Robert Frost.
> Maya wrote a story called "The Unbelievable Day of Penelope P. Pepper."

> **Tip**
> Titles of books, movies, and plays may be set in italics when they are in print.
> Have you read the book *Beetles, Lightly Toasted*?

**Identify It**

Read each sentence below. Underline the titles of books, movies, and plays. Put quotation marks around the titles of songs, stories, and poems.

1. If you like animal movies, you will probably like <u>Homeward Bound</u> and <u>The Adventures of Milo and Otis</u>.

2. My cousin knows all the songs in the play <u>Fiddler on the Roof</u>.

3. At preschool, my little sister learned the song "Itsy Bitsy Spider."

4. Manvel ordered <u>Tuck Everlasting</u> from an online bookstore.

5. Devon saw the play <u>Aladdin and the Magic Lamp</u> in New York.

6. John Agard wrote a poem called "Catch Me a Riddle."

**88**

**Rewrite It**

Rewrite each sentence below. Titles should be underlined or placed in quotation marks, as necessary.

1. Why Do Heroes Have Big Feet? is a play based on tall tales of the Midwest.

   <u>Why Do Heroes Have Big Feet?</u> is a play based on tall tales of the Midwest.

2. The Rum Tum Tugger by T. S. Eliot is my father's favorite poem.

   "The Rum Tum Tugger" by T. S. Eliot is my father's favorite poem.

3. My favorite story in the book A Classic Treasury of Aesop's Fables is called The City Mouse and the Country Mouse.

   My favorite story in the book <u>A Classic Treasury of Aesop's Fables</u> is called "The City Mouse and the Country Mouse."

4. Mom rented two DVDs: Lilo and Stitch, and Ella Enchanted.

   Mom rented two DVDs: <u>Lilo and Stitch,</u> and <u>Ella Enchanted.</u>

**Try It**

Answer the following questions using complete sentences.

1. What is your favorite book, and who is the author?

   _____

2. What is the funni_____ ever read?

   **Answers will vary.**

89

---

Use a **colon between the hour and the minute** when there is a reference to a specific time. There should not be a space before or after the colon.
   6:30 A.M.   7:27 P.M.   at 10:45 last night   9:00–5:00 every day

Use a **colon before a list of items**. The words before the colon must be a complete sentence. Put one space after the colon before you begin the list.
   You will need the following ingredients: sugar, flour, eggs, vanilla, and butter.
   The kit included these items: instructions, screws, small nails, wood glue, and four wooden shelves.

**Complete It**

Read each sentence below. If the sentence is correct, make a check mark on the line. If it is not correct, make an **X** on the line. Then, add colons where they are needed.

1. __X__ Eva identified the following birds at her birdfeeder: robins, blue jays, cardinals, chickadees, sparrows, tufted titmice, and woodpeckers.

2. __X__ Here are the ingredients you will need to make your own ginger-soda: honey, apple cider vinegar, carbonated water, and sliced fresh ginger.

3. __X__ The first flight arrives at 6:15, and the next one arrives at 10:06.

4. __✓__ Marcus's best friends are Kevin, James, Rebekah, and Jada.

5. __X__ We will need the following items to make granola: oats, almonds, honey, sunflower seeds, puffed rice cereal, cinnamon, canola oil, and dried fruit.

6. __✓__ Kickoff is at 2:30 on Saturday afternoon.

90

---

**Proof It**

Read the day planner below. Some colons are used incorrectly and others are missing. Add or delete colons where necessary.

| ᴇ – deletes punctuation |
| ⟨ – inserts colon |

**Week of March 7–13**

| Monday, March 7 | Doctor appointment at 12:15 |
| Tuesday, March 8 | Meeting with Mrs. Klum 4:00–4:45 |
| Wednesday, March 9 | Stop at the grocery store for: milk, wheat bread, Swiss cheese, cereal, and oranges. |
| Thursday, March 10 | Send invitations to the following families: the Kobelts, the O'Malleys, and the Jiangs. |
| Friday, March 11 | Call the following businesses to see if they will donate to the school auction: Blendon's Bakery, Booktown, and Harris Market. |
| Saturday, March 12 | Cameron's soccer game at 12:30 |
| Sunday, March 13 | Free kids' concert at McGregor Park 1:00–3:00 |

**Try It**

Use a colon and a complete sentence in your answer to each question.

1. What are three ingredients needed to make your favorite dinner?

   _____

2. Imagine that you_____ at are four things you would need to bring with you?

   **Answers will vary.**

91

---

**Quotation marks** are used before and after **dialogue**, or the exact words a person says. If the dialogue does not end the sentence, but would normally take a period, put a comma inside the quotation marks and a period at the end of the sentence.
   "I have a dream today," said Dr. King in his famous speech.

If the dialogue ends with a question mark or an exclamation point, place the end mark inside the quotation marks. Place a period at the end of the entire sentence.
   "Who invented chewing gum?" asked Ian.

If part of the sentence comes before the dialogue, put a comma after that part of the sentence. Put the end mark inside the quotation marks.
   Natasha asked, "What time will the bus arrive?"

**Titles of books, movies, and plays** may be underlined or italicized. **Titles of songs, poems, and stories** are set in quotation marks.
   <u>Coyotes in the Crosswalk</u> is a book about animals in cities.
   Hailey knows most of the words to the song "Catch the Moon."

Use a **colon between the hour and the minute**.
   8:36 A.M.        2:20 P.M.        every day at 6:15

Use a **colon before a list of items** if the words before the colon are a complete sentence.
   Bring the following items: a sketchbook, paints, and two brushes.

**Putting It Together**

Complete each sentence below with a title. Use correct punctuation.

1. My favorite animated movie is _____.

2. I think that _____ e a great story title.

   **Answers will vary.**

3. _____ is the funniest book I know.

92

---

# Answer Key

---

Read each pair of sentences below. Circle the
letter of the sentence that is written correctly.

1. **a.** The pool is open from 10:0 until 50:0.
   **(b.)** The pool is open from 1:00 until 5:00.

2. **a.** "It's Raining Pigs and Noodles" is a book of poetry by Jack Prelutsky.
   **(b.)** *It's Raining Pigs and Noodles* is a book of poetry by Jack Prelutsky.

3. **(a.)** In the box, there were two books, three CDs, and a photo.
   **b.** In the box, there were: two books, three CDs, and a photo.

4. **(a.)** The last showing of the movie *Robots* is at 7:40.
   **b.** The last showing of the movie "Robots" is at 7 40.

Proofread the passage below. Add or
delete quotation marks and punctuation
as needed.

| | |
|---|---|
| ℓ | – deletes punctuation |
| ⋎ | – inserts quotations |
| ∧ | – inserts punctuation |

Lea and Elizabeth carefully unlatched the trunk Elizabeth found in

attic. "This must have been Mom's dress when she was just a baby," said

Lea, unfolding a tiny blue dress. "I can't believe how tiny she was!"

Elizabeth asked "Did you see all these old books?" She pulled out the

following books and stacked them on the table All-of-a-Kind Family, Little

Women, Anne of Green Gables, and A Child's Garden of Verses.

Lea read the poems Bed in Summer and Land of Counterpane out

loud. We should ask Mom if she read to us from this book when we were

little," said Lea. "I know I've heard these poems before."

93

---

When the subject of a sentence is singular, the verb usually ends with **s** or
**es**.

Add **s** to most regular verbs that have a single subject.
   *Phoebe jumps* rope.          *The tiger races* across the savanna.

Add **es** to regular verbs that have a single subject and end in **o**, **sh**, **ch**, **s**,
**x**, and **z**.
   *Dad washes* the dinner dishes.
   *Corey coaxes* the kitten from her hiding place.

If the verb ends in **y**, drop the **y** and add **ies**.
   *We worry* about the storm.   *Will worries* about the storm.

When the subject is plural, the verb does not end with **s** or **es**.
   *Akiko and Dustin live* in the same apartment building.
   *The puppies play* with the rubber toy.

**Complete It**
Read the paragraph below. Circle the verb from the pair in parentheses
that correctly completes each sentence.

Joseph Malarkey (invent, (invents)) things. He ((thinks), think) of amazing
and interesting ideas. Then, he (try, (tries)) to create his inventions. Some of
them are great successes, and others are not. Joseph has a twin sister
named Josefina. Joseph and Josefina ((work), works) on many inventions
together. For example, they (invents, (invent)) amazing new recycling
machines. You (places, (place)) cans inside the machine. It (wash, (washes))
and ((dries), dry) the cans, and then it ((crushes), crush) them into incredibly
tiny pieces. Joseph (push, (pushes)) the big green button. The pieces ((whirl),
whirls) inside the machine. In moments, the machine (produce, (produces))
a brand-new, shiny toy car!

94

---

**Proof It**
Read the sentences below. Make sure the
subject and the verb, or verbs, agree in
each sentence. Correct the mistakes you
find using proofreading marks.

| | |
|---|---|
| ℓ | – deletes punctuation |
| ∧ | – inserts punctuation |

1. Every summer, Eduardo and Crista catches tadpoles in Miller Creek.
   *es*

2. Crista toss the net into the mucky water.
   *es*

3. Eduardo stand nearby and hold a jar filled with creek water.
   *s*        *s*

4. Eduardo and Crista brings home the tadpoles.

5. Crista supply the tadpoles with food, water, and places to hide.
   *ies*

6. Over time, the tadpoles grows legs and loses their gills and tail.

7. The children watches the curious creatures change into frogs.

8. They carefully carries the young frogs back to Miller Creek.

9. Eduardo and Crista releases the frogs at the edge of the creek and
   watches as they hops away.

**Try It**

1. Write a sentence about something you do every summer. Underline
   the subject, and circle the verb.

   _____

2. Now, use a plura[...]  Answers will vary.  [...]about something that
   people do every winter. Underline the subject, and circle the verb.

   _____

95

---

**Past-tense verbs** tell about things that have already
happened. To change most regular verbs to the past
tense, add **ed**. If the verb already ends in **e**, just add **d**.
   Chase *wanted* a green balloon.
   The movers *lifted* the boxes into the truck.
   Melanie *skated* around the pond.

If a verb ends in **y**, change the **y** to **i** and add **ed**.
   The nurses *apply* pressure to the wound.
   The nurses *applied* pressure to the wound.

**Identify It**
Read the sentences below. Circle the present-tense verb in each
sentence. Then, write the past tense of the verb on the line.

1. _____served_____ Eleanor Roosevelt (serves) as First Lady from 1933
   until 1945.

2. _____believed_____ She (believes) in human rights for all people.

3. _____supported_____ She (supports) the Civil Rights Movement.

4. _____studied_____ As a teenager, Eleanor (studies) at a London
   boarding school.

5. _____married_____ Eleanor and Franklin Roosevelt (marry) in 1905.

6. _____visited_____ During World War I, Eleanor (visits) wounded
   soldiers.

7. _____created_____ Later, she (creates) programs for children, women,
   and minorities.

8. _____enjoyed_____ In her spare time, Eleanor (enjoys) traveling and
   archery.

96

---

## Complete It

Read the sentences below. Complete each sentence with the past tense of the verb in parentheses.

1. New Yorkers **elected** Hillary Clinton to the Senate while she was still First Lady. (elect)

2. Abigail Adams's grandson **published** the letters she wrote to her husband, President Adams. (publish)

3. Grace Coolidge **worked** as a teacher of hearing-impaired children. (work)

4. Lady Bird Johnson **traveled** to 33 foreign countries as wife of the vice-president. (travel)

5. Laura Bush **studied** library science at the University of Texas. (study)

6. Edith Roosevelt **loved** books and reading. (love)

7. As first lady, Rosalynn Carter **tried** to bring attention to the performing arts. (try)

8. Lou Hoover **enjoyed** camping, hunting, riding horses, and geology. (enjoy)

## Try It

Write two sentences in the present tense on a separate sheet of paper. Be sure to use regular verbs in your sentences. Rewrite your sentences in the past tense on the lines below.

1. _____

2. _____

Answers will vary.

**97**

---

The **past tense** of some verbs is irregular. Instead of adding **ed** or **d** to form the past tenses of these verbs, you need to memorize the past-tense forms.

| Present Tense | Past Tense |
|---|---|
| the leaves *fall* | the leaves *fell* |
| the chipmunks *dig* | the chipmunks *dug* |
| the story *begins* | the story *began* |
| we *take* the dog | we *took* the dog |
| Dad *sings* | Dad *sang* |

## Complete It

Each pair of sentences below is written in the past and the present tense. Fill in the spaces with past- or present-tense verbs to complete the sentences.

1. Present Tense: Everyone **sings** the National Anthem.
   Past Tense: Everyone sang the National Anthem.

2. Present Tense: The archaeologists dig for clues.
   Past Tense: The archaeologists **dug** for clues.

3. Present Tense: Adam takes some herbs from the garden.
   Past Tense: Adam **took** some herbs from the garden.

4. Present Tense: The day begins with the beeping alarm.
   Past Tense: The day **began** with the beeping alarm.

5. Present Tense: Mrs. Bickleton falls on a patch of ice.
   Past Tense: Mrs. Bickleton **fell** on a patch of ice.

6. Present Tense: Lulu **digs** a hole for the chestnut tree.
   Past Tense: Lulu dug a hole for the chestnut tree.

7. Present Tense: The movie **begins** with a funny scene.
   Past Tense: The movie began with a funny scene.

**98**

---

## Solve It

Read each sentence below. Circle the verb. In the space, write the past tense of the verb. Then, find each past-tense verb in the word search puzzle.

1. The mole (digs) its tunnel far beneath the garden.
   **dug**

2. The dead tree (falls) with an enormous crash. **fell**

3. Mom (sings) the same lullaby to my baby brother every night.
   **sang**

4. The concert (begins) at 8:00.
   **began**

5. Annabelle (takes) violin lessons.
   **took**

| g | f | j | d | e | s | w |
|---|---|---|---|---|---|---|
| h | n | f | u | d | a | m |
| o | b | e | g | a | n | k |
| e | d | l | q | i | g | c |
| b | r | l | t | o | o | k |
| s | f | j | a | d | y | p |

## Try It

Write a short paragraph on the lines below. Use the past tense of three of the following verbs in your paragraph: *fall, dig, begin, take,* or *sing.*

Answers will vary.

**99**

---

The **past tense** of some verbs is irregular. Instead of adding **ed** or **d** to form the past tenses of these verbs, you need to memorize the past-tense forms.

| Present Tense | Past Tense |
|---|---|
| we *speak* | we *spoke* |
| Doug *draws* | Doug *drew* |
| the egg *breaks* | the egg *broke* |
| Amelia *catches* | Amelia *caught* |
| we *leave* | we *left* |

## Rewrite It

The sentences below are all in the present tense. Rewrite them in the past tense.

1. The Howards accidentally leave the back window open.
   **The Howards accidentally left the back window open.**

2. They catch a confused bat flying around the house.
   **They caught a confused bat flying around the house.**

3. Mr. Howard breaks a vase sitting on the fireplace mantel.
   **Mr. Howard broke a vase sitting on the fireplace mantel.**

4. Lara Howard draws a picture of the bat for her afternoon art class.
   **Lara Howard drew a picture of the bat for her afternoon art class.**

5. Mrs. Howard speaks with the bat expert at the Nature Center.
   **Mrs. Howard spoke with the bat expert at the Nature Center.**

**100**

---

---

**Proof It**

Read the diary entry below. Find the seven verbs that are in the wrong tense or that are spelled incorrectly. Use proofreading marks to correct the mistakes.

> ⌐ – deletes words or letters
> ∧ – inserts words or letters

Sunday, August 22

Dear Diary,

    It has been a crazy week! I ~~catched~~ *caught* a cold just a few days before we ~~leaved~~ *left* for the family reunion. Luckily, it lasted for only two days. Dad ~~speaked~~ *spoke* to Uncle Albert on the phone. He told Dad that more than 40 members of our family would be coming to this reunion!

    We ~~catch~~ *caught* the train at 8:00 on Friday morning. We almost missed it because two wheels on Mom's suitcase ~~breaked~~ *broke*. There wasn't time to fix them, so we had to run for the train carrying the suitcase. Dad ~~speaks~~ *spoke* to the ticket agent, and he held the train for us. The train ~~leaves~~ *left* the station at 8:06, and we were on our way to the Delregno family reunion in Boston!

**Try It**

The verb *catch* can be used in several different ways. On the lines below, write two sentences in the past tense about different things you can catch.

> Answers will vary.

101

---

When the subject of a sentence is singular, the verb usually ends with **s** or **es**. Add **s** to regular verbs that have a singular subject. Add **es** if the verb ends with **o**, **sh**, **ch**, **s**, **x**, or **z**.

> Austin *swims* at the community pool.    Mason *pitches* the ball.

If the verb ends in **y**, drop the **y** and add **ies**.

> They always *hurry* in the morning.  He always *hurries* in the morning.

When the subject is plural, the verb does not end with **s** or **es**.

> The fans *cheer* for their favorite players.

To change most regular verbs to the past tense, add **ed**. If the verb already ends in **e**, just add **d**.

> The scientist *discovered* a cure.    Matt *raked* the leaves.

If a verb ends in **y**, change the **y** to **i** and add **ed**.

> Bailey and Scott *cry* at the movie.    Bailey *cried* at the movie.

The past tenses of some verbs are irregular. Instead of adding **ed** or **d**, you need to memorize the past-tense forms.

| | | |
|---|---|---|
| fall → fell | speak → spoke | dig → dug |
| draw → drew | begin → began | break → broke |
| take → took | catch → caught | sing → sang |
| leave → left | | |

**Putting It Together**

Read each sentence below. Then, circle the verb from the pair in parentheses that best completes each sentence.

1. The opossum (waddle, **waddles**) across the street.
2. The raccoons (**look**, looks) for food in the trashcan.
3. A bat (**flies**, fly) across the sky at twilight.

102

---

The verbs in bold are in the present tense. Write the past-tense form of each verb on the line.

1. The moonflower **blooms** in the middle of the night.   **bloomed**
2. The bushbaby **leaps** from branch to branch in the bright moonlight.   **leaped**
3. Late at night, the skunk **digs** in the garden in search of insects.   **dug**
4. Debbie **plants** an evening primrose next to her bedroom window.   **planted**
5. The whippoorwill **catches** insects as they flew through the night air.   **caught**
6. I fell asleep as the crickets **sing** in the summer evening.   **sang**
7. Dozens of moths **gather** around the bright porch light.   **gathered**

Read the clues below. Write the answers in the numbered spaces in the crossword puzzle.

Across
2 past tense of *whisper*
4 past tense of *leave*
5 present tense of *broke*
7 past tense of *discover*

Down
1 past tense of *carry*
2 past tense of *worry*
3 past tense of *speak*
6 present tense of *fried*

Crossword answers: whispered, left, break, discovered, carried, worried, spoke, fry

103

---

There are three main verb tenses: the past tense, the present tense, and the future tense. The **past tense** describes things that have already happened. The **present tense** describes things that are happening right now. The **future tense** describes something that will take place in the future.

> **Past:** The members of the band *marched* down Main Street.
> **Present:** The members of the band *march* down Main Street.
> **Future:** The members of the band *will march* down Main Street.

Form the future tense by using the word *will* with a verb.

> The library **will** *close* at 5:00.    The pretzels **will** *bake* for 35 minutes.
> Andre **will** *graduate* in June.    Zan **will** *draw* your portrait.

**Identify It**

Read each sentence below. If it is in the future tense, make a check mark on the line. If it is not, write the future tense of the verb on the line.

1.   ✓   Twenty years from now, life will be very different.
2. **will make** Every day, scientists and inventors make new discoveries.
3.   ✓   Refrigerators of the future will be smart, according to scientists.
4. **will tell; will need** They tell you what ingredients you need to make a certain dish.
5.   ✓   These amazing refrigerators will even help you plan a balanced diet!
6. **will rely** People rely on computers for many things every day.
7.   ✓   Computers and tiny radio transmitters will create smarter kitchens in the future.

104

**Rewrite It**

In the space before each sentence, write **PA** if the sentence takes place in the past. Write **PR** if it takes place in the present. Then, rewrite each sentence in the future tense.

1. _PR_ Clothes of the future have many interesting features.

   Clothes of the future will have many interesting features.

2. _PR_ They are made of a special kind of material.

   They will be made of a special kind of material.

3. _PR_ This incredible new material always stays dry and clean.

   This incredible new material will always stay dry and clean.

4. _PA_ Another type of material contained tiny electric fibers.

   Another type of material will contain tiny electric fibers.

5. _PA_ People listened to their clothes like radios.

   People will listen to their clothes like radios.

6. _PR_ The clothes even change color and patterns.

   The clothes will even change color and patterns.

**Try It**

Use your imagination to think of an invention that could make life easier for people of the future. Write a short paragraph in the future tense that describes what your invention will do.

Answers will vary.

105

---

Certain verbs are easily confused with one another. Sometimes, using these words correctly takes a little bit of extra thought.

The verb *lie* can mean *to rest in a flat position*. The past tense of *lie* is *lay*.
   Ryan has a headache, so he is going to *lie* down.
   Ryan *lay* on the bed until he felt better.
*Lay* can also mean *to put or place*. The past tense of *lay* is *laid*.
   Mia *lay* the papers down.          Mia *laid* the papers down.

The verb *sit* means *to be in a seated position*. The past tense of *sit* is *sat*.
   Ethan *sits* on the front stoop.          Ethan *sat* on the front stoop.
*Set* can mean *to put or place*. The past and present tense are the same.
   I *set* the table.          Yesterday, I *set* the table.

*Can* means *able to*. *May* means *allowed to*.
   I *can* juggle six balls. (I *am able to* juggle six balls)
   You *may* stay up until midnight on New Year's Eve. (You *are allowed to* stay up.)

**Complete It**

Underline the word in parentheses that correctly completes each sentence.

1. Imani (set, sat) at a table in the Make It and Bake It Pottery Studio.

2. She (lied, laid) out all the paints she planned to use.

3. "(May, Can) I use these paintbrushes?" Imani asked Jenna, the owner.

4. Jenna nodded. "I will (sit, set) them here so you can reach them."

5. "I (may, can) paint flowers, but people are harder, "said Imani.

6. When Imani was done, Jenna (set, sat) the dishes in the kiln to bake.

106

---

**Proof It**

Read the sentences below. Use proofreading marks to correct the eight verbs that are used incorrectly.

| | |
|---|---|
| ✎ | – deletes words or letters |
| ʌ | – inserts words or letters |

   Imani carried the painted bowl and flowerpot into her room. She carefully ~~sat~~ *set* them on a high shelf in her closet. Suddenly, there was a knock on her door. Imani quickly ~~laid~~ *lay* down on her bed and pretended to look at a book.

   "~~Can~~ *May* I come in?" asked Imani's mom, opening the door a crack.

   "Sure," said Imani. Her mom ~~set~~ *laid* a stack of neatly folded laundry on the dresser and ~~set~~ *sat* down on the bed.

   "Do you feel okay?" she asked. "It's not like you to come home and ~~lay~~ *lie* down right away."

   "I feel fine," replied Imani, ~~setting~~ *sitting* up. "I was just a little tired this afternoon. I ~~may~~ *can* put away my own laundry," she added quickly, when she saw her mom heading for the closet.

   "Phew," said Imani, as her mom went back downstairs a moment later. "I need to find a better hiding place for my pottery. Mom's birthday is still a week away!"

107

---

**Past**, **present**, and **future** are the three main verb tenses. They are used to refer to things that have already happened, that are happening right now, and that will happen in the future.

Form the **future tense** by using the word *will* with a verb.
   The baby-sitter *will* be here soon.
   Bethany *will* read your story.

Some words are easily confused with one another. Refer to the examples below if you need help remembering which word to use.
   *lie* = to rest in a flat position (past tense is *lay*)
   *lay* = to put or place (past tense is *laid*)
   *sit* = to be in a seated position (past tense is *sat*)
   *set* = to put or place (past tense is *set*)
   *can* = able to          *may* = allowed to

**Putting It Together**

Complete each sentence below with a word from the box.

| lie | lay | laid | sit | sat | set | can | may |
|---|---|---|---|---|---|---|---|

1. Mr. Damian put down his briefcase and __laid/set__ the mail on the table.

2. You __may__ have some pudding when you finish your dinner.

3. If you __lie__ down on the paper, I can trace the outline of your body.

4. Sabrina __sat__ on the porch step and waited for the rain to stop.

5. George __can__ do 25 push-ups.

6. Please __set__ the can of paint on the newspapers.

108

---

---

Read the sentences below, and circle the verbs. Write *past*, *present*, or *future* on the line to show the verb tense.

1. The Winter Olympics (occur) every four years. **present**

2. The first Olympic Games (were held) in 1896 in Athens, Greece. **past**

3. The Summer Games and the Winter Games (are held) in different years. **present**

4. The 2008 Summer Games (will be) in Beijing, China. **future**

5. Vancouver, Canada, (will host) the 2010 Winter Olympics. **future**

6. The Olympic flag (shows) five linked rings in blue, yellow, black, green, and red. **present**

7. The flag (was used) for the first time in 1920 in Antwerp, Belgium. **past**

Complete each sentence with the future tense of the verb in parentheses.

1. Who **will light** the Olympic Flame at the 2012 Olympics? (light)

2. Thousands of people **will travel** to China to see the athletes perform. (travel)

3. No one knows which country **will bring** home the most gold medals. (bring)

4. Do you think the Olympics **will come** to your hometown one day? (come)

5. Do you think that sports like golf, bowling, and surfing **will be** Olympic sports someday? (be)

**109**

---

A **contraction** is a short way of writing or saying something. When you combine two words in a contraction, an apostrophe (') takes the place of the missing letters.

Often, pronouns and verbs are combined in contractions.
*She is* taking the subway.   *She's* taking the subway.
*They will* ski the difficult slopes.   *They'll* ski the difficult slopes.

Contractions can also be formed with verbs and the word *not*.
Dallas *is not* the capital of Texas.   Dallas *isn't* the capital of Texas.
Lorenzo *does not* like mushrooms.   Lorenzo *doesn't* like mushrooms.

> **Tip**
> In a question, the two words that can form a contraction may not be next to one another.
> Why *could* you *not* arrive on time?
> Why *couldn't* you arrive on time?

**Rewrite It**
Rewrite each sentence below using contractions. The number in parentheses will tell you how many contractions to use.

1. Have Charley and Tess not visited New York City before? (1)
   **Haven't Charley and Tess visited New York City before?**

2. They will go to Times Square and Grand Central Station. (1)
   **They'll go to Times Square and Grand Central Station.**

3. They have planned a spring trip, so it will not be cold outside. (2)
   **They've planned a spring trip, so it won't be cold outside.**

4. I have asked for a souvenir from the Empire State Building. (1)
   **I've asked for a souvenir from the Empire State Building.**

**110**

---

**Proof It**
Read the paragraphs below. Six contractions contain mistakes. Use proofreading marks to correct the mistakes.

> ⌐ - deletes punctuation
> ↓ - inserts apostrophe

Manhattan's Central Park is one of the most famous parks in the world. For New Yorkers, there just isn't any place like it. New York City is covered with buildings and skyscrapers as far as the eye can see. People don't have to leave the city to find green space, though. The park rests on 843 acres of land. Human visitors aren't the only ones to enjoy this green oasis in the city. Birds, bugs, and small mammals make their homes there. They're easy to spot on a walk through the park.

Many people enjoy the sculptures of Central Park. Frederick Olmsted, one of the park's designers, didn't want sculptures in the park. He thought it would look cluttered. Today, the sculptures are a part of the park, and most people can't imagine it without them.

**Try It**
Combine words from the boxes below to form contractions. Write two sentences using the contractions.

| I | he | it | they | can | not | have | is | would |
|---|----|----|------|-----|-----|------|----|----|
| you | she | we | could | did | will | am | are | |

1. _____
2. _____   Answers will vary.

**111**

---

Words such as *no, none, never, nothing, nobody, nowhere,* and *no one* are **negative words**. The word *not* and contractions with *not* are also negative words. **Double negatives** are sentences with more than one negative word. Do not use double negatives in your writing.

| Incorrect | Correct |
|-----------|---------|
| There *isn't nothing* left. | There *isn't* anything left. |
| | There is *nothing* left. |
| Kris did *not* bring *no* CDs. | Kris did *not* bring any CDs. |
| | Kris brought *no* CDs. |

**Complete It**
Underline the word in parentheses that correctly completes each sentence.

1. I haven't (<u>ever</u>, never) written a letter to the state governor before.

2. I will tell Governor Hernandez that there (isn't, <u>is</u>) nowhere in the state as polluted as Dandelion River.

3. No one can (never, <u>ever</u>) swim or go boating or fishing in the river.

4. There isn't (no, <u>any</u>) reason why companies should be allowed to keep polluting the river.

5. Nobody has ever made the companies do (nothing, <u>anything</u>) to clean up the water.

6. Pollution (<u>has</u>, hasn't) not always been a problem in Dandelion River.

> **Tip**
> The two negatives in a double negative cancel each other out.
> *I don't want no ice cream* actually means *I do want ice cream.*

**112**

---

## Page 113

**Proof It**

There are five double negatives in the letter below. Find each double negative, and correct it using proofreading marks.

> ℓ – deletes words
> ʌ – inserts words

April 14

Dear Governor Hernandez,

My name is Alysha Aroya. I am writing to you because I am concerned about Dandelion River. The river was once beautiful. It was a part of my parents' childhoods. Today, no one can't use the river for recreation. Fish and other wildlife cannot live there no longer. People throw litter in the water because they think no one will never do anything to save the river. They believe it's a lost cause.

As long as the big companies *[Answers will vary.]* change, the river will stay polluted. They shouldn't never be allowed to do so much damage to the environment.

I am enclosing a list of 100 signatures. The people who signed their names know how important it is to clean up Dandelion River. We hope that you agree and help us make a positive change.

Sincerely,

Alysha Aroya

**Try It**

Write a short paragraph about something in your town or state that you think is worth saving, such as a building or natural area. Correctly use at least three negative words in your writing.

*Answers will vary.*

## Page 114

When you combine two words to form a **contraction**, an apostrophe takes the place of the missing letters.

*I am* in the fifth grade. — *I'm* in the fifth grade.
*He will* forget to bring his lunch. — *He'll* forget to bring his lunch.
Pandas *are not* really bears. — Pandas *aren't* really bears.

*No, none, never, nothing, nobody, nowhere, no one,* and contractions with *not* are **negative words**. Never use a **double negative**, or two negatives together.
**Incorrect:** There *weren't no* free samples left.
**Correct:** There *weren't* any free samples left.
**Correct:** There *were no* free samples left.

**Putting It Together**

On the line, write a contraction for each pair of underlined words.

1. **wasn't** — Mark Twain <u>was not</u> the real name of the famous Missouri author.
2. **haven't** — Even if you <u>have not</u> read Twain's books, you might have heard of Tom Sawyer.
3. **You'll** — <u>You will</u> probably enjoy reading all about Tom's many adventures.
4. **isn't** — The Adventures of Tom Sawyer <u>is not</u> Twain's only famous book.
5. **didn't** — Twain <u>did not</u> write only fiction stories.
6. **would've** — He <u>would have</u> loved to spend all his days on the Mississippi River.
7. **doesn't** — It might be hard to find a riverboat pilot who <u>does not</u> know all about fellow pilot Mark Twain.

## Page 115

Circle the word in parentheses that correctly completes each sentence.

1. The Mississippi River (**is**/ isn't) not the longest river in the United States.
2. Historians believe there were not (**any**/ no) Europeans who reached the river before Hernando de Soto in 1541.
3. There was not (nothing/ **anything**) as exciting as the steamboat races on the river in the mid-1800s.
4. If you travel to New Orleans, Memphis, or St. Louis, you (**will**/ won't) not be far from the mighty Mississippi.
5. No one had (never/ **ever**) swum the entire length of the river before Martin Strel in 2002.

Read the paragraph below. Seven contractions contain mistakes. Use proofreading marks to correct the mistakes.

> ℓ – deletes punctuation
> ↓ – inserts apostrophe

My uncle, Beau, wants to travel down the Mississippi River by raft, just like Mark Twain's Huck Finn. He's planning the trip with several of his friends. They're going to make the raft themselves. I think it's amazing that they found instructions for building a raft on the Internet. Captain Benjamin Lee Adams will pilot the raft. He's been a riverboat pilot for more than 30 years. My parents were a little worried that Uncle Beau didn't know what he was getting into. They're relieved that someone with so much experience will be going on the adventure. Uncle Beau says this will be the experience of a lifetime. I hope he isn't disappointed!

## Page 116

*Singular* means *one*. *Plural* means *more than one*. To change a regular noun from singular to plural, add **s**.
Singular: workbook dinosaur tractor
Plural: workbook**s** dinosaur**s** tractor**s**

If a noun ends in **sh**, **ch**, **s**, or **x**, form the plural by adding **es**.
Singular: beach flash boss tax
Plural: beach**es** flash**es** boss**es** tax**es**

If a noun ends with a consonant and a **y**, form the plural by dropping the **y** and adding **ies**.
Singular: cherry baby diary lady penny
Plural: cherr**ies** bab**ies** diar**ies** lad**ies** penn**ies**

For most nouns that end in **f** or **fe**, form the plural by changing the **f** or **fe** to **ve** and adding **s**.
Singular: shelf leaf knife hoof wife
Plural: shel**ves** lea**ves** kni**ves** hoo**ves** wi**ves**

**Match It**

Match each singular word to its plural form. Write the letter of your answer on the line.

1. **a** enemy — a. enemies — b. enemys
2. **b** wish — a. wishs — b. wishes
3. **b** sunflower — a. sunfloweres — b. sunflowers
4. **b** duty — a. duteys — b. duties
5. **a** wolf — a. wolves — b. wolfs
6. **b** helicopter — a. helicopteres — b. helicopters
7. **a** loaf — a. loaves — b. loafs

## Page 117

**Proof It**
Read the paragraphs below. Nine plural words are spelled incorrectly. Use proofreading marks to correct them.

> ℰ – deletes words or letters
> ^ – inserts words or letters

The Chinese New Year occurs sometime between January 21 and February 19. The exact date depends on the cycles of the moon. The party and celebrations last for about two weeks.

Cities and towns are decorated with flowers and paper lanterns in bright colors. People eat special holiday foods. For example, seafood, dumplings, noodles, and pastry with seeds are common New Year's dishs. Married couples often give small red packets, or pouchs, as gifts to friends and relatives. These packets usually contain money and are meant to be a sign of good fortune in the coming year.

Dragon dances are a part of the celebrations. As many as 50 people might wear a single costume. Fireworks, dragon dances, and other New Year's traditions can be found in Chinatowns across the United States.

**Try It**
Write a short paragraph describing a holiday that you and your family celebrate. Use at least four plural words.

> Answers will vary.

**117**

## Page 118

Some plural words are irregular and do not follow the rules. For example, to form the plural of words that end in **o**, you add **s** or **es**. You must memorize the forms of irregular plurals.

| Singular: | kangaroo | piano | studio | solo | auto |
| --- | --- | --- | --- | --- | --- |
| Plural: | kangaroos | pianos | studios | solos | autos |

| Singular: | tomato | echo | hero | potato |
| --- | --- | --- | --- | --- |
| Plural: | tomatoes | echoes | heroes | potatoes |

For some words, the plural form is totally different than the singular form.
man → men    foot → feet    louse → lice    ox → oxen
goose → geese    mouse → mice    tooth → teeth    die → dice
child → children    woman → women

The singular and plural forms of the following words are the same: *deer, fish, moose, sheep, trout, salmon, cod, series, species, traffic, wheat,* and *offspring.*

**Identify It**
Choose the correct version of each sentence below and circle it.

1. a. Buy one pound of tomatos.
   **b.** Buy one pound of tomatoes.

2. **a.** How many species of toads are there?
   b. How many specieses of toads are there?

3. **a.** Six oxen pulled the cart.
   b. Six oxes pulled the cart.

4. a. The box can hold photoes or videoes.
   **b.** The box can hold photos or videos.

5. **a.** Which of these radios sounds best?
   b. Which of these radioes sounds best?

**118**

## Page 119

**Solve It**
Complete each sentence below with the plural form of the word in parentheses. Use a dictionary if you need help. Then, search for each plural word in the puzzle.

| s | a | h | p | n | a | t | r | o |
| f | g | v | w | q | t | a | o | n |
| r | h | c | h | i | l | d | r | e | n |
| b | a | k | e | z | j | l | p | i | p |
| w | p | i | a | n | o | s | e | f | n |
| v | e | u | t | d | s | f | d | b | o |
| r | t | n | a | p | t | r | o | u | t |
| q | l | x | u | f | a | y | e | j | n |
| p | o | t | a | t | o | e | s | f | k |

1. The movers carefully carried two _____**pianos**_____ up a steep flight of stairs. (piano)

2. How many _____**children**_____ will be at the picnic? (child)

3. Michi and her dad caught three rainbow _____**trout**_____ when they went to the lake. (trout)

4. The tour guide showed us several _____**torpedoes**_____ that were used in World War II. (torpedo)

5. The field of _____**wheat**_____ looked golden in the sun. (wheat)

6. We grew _____**potatoes**_____, zucchini, and peppers. (potato)

**Try It**
Write two sentences using the plural forms of at least two of the following words: *man, hero, woman, deer, auto, photo, potato, mouse, sheep, zoo.*

> Answers will vary.

**119**

## Page 120

To form the **possessive** of a singular noun, add an apostrophe (') and the letter **s** to the end of the word. This indicates that the person or thing is the owner of the object that follows the possessive.

the boat**'s** deck    the telescope**'s** lens    Malik**'s** vacation
Nissa**'s** party    the pig**'s** trough    Ms. Nilsson**'s** flowers

**Complete It**
Write the possessive form of each noun in parentheses to complete the sentences below.

1. _____**Jane Goodall's**_____ job is to study chimpanzees in the wild. (Jane Goodall)

2. This _____**zoologist's**_____ work has broken new ground in the study of animals and science. (zoologist)

3. _____**Jane's**_____ discovery that chimpanzees make and use tools was very important. (Jane)

4. The _____**chimp's**_____ behavior often amuses and surprises Jane. (chimp)

5. Jane has watched _____**Fifi's**_____ nine children grow up. (Fifi)

6. Jane and her husband studied other African animals on _____**Tanzania's**_____ Serengeti Plain. (Tanzania)

7. Her _____**life's**_____ work has been to preserve wild animals and places. (life)

**120**

**Rewrite It**

Rewrite each sentence below. Replace the words in parentheses with a possessive.

1. (The books of the scientist) describe her experiences at Gombe National Park.

   The scientist's books describe her experiences at Gombe National Park.

2. Jane gives much credit to (the encouragement of her mother).

   Jane gives much credit to her mother's encouragement.

3. (The face of a chimp) can show emotions like joy, fear, sadness, surprise, and amusement.

   A chimp's face can show emotions like joy, fear, sadness, surprise, and amusement.

4. (The rain forests of Africa) make a good home for chimps, but they are quickly disappearing.

   Africa's rain forests make a good home for chimps, but they are quickly disappearing.

**Try It**

Write a sentence about a person who has an interesting career. Use a possessive in your sentence.

Answers will vary.

121

---

To form the **possessive of a plural word** that ends in **s**, add an apostrophe after the **s**.

| the flags' colors | the athletes' equipment |
| the computers' screens | the cars' engines |
| the students' homework | the birds' feathers |

For plural words that do not end in **s**, add an apostrophe and an **s** to form the possessive.

the teeth**'s** size    the people**'s** ideas    the women**'s** clothing

Do not mistake a plural for a possessive. Possessives always have an apostrophe.

Plural:     trees      zebras       the Johnsons
Possessive: trees' leaves  zebras' stripes  the Johnsons' apartment

**Identify It**

Read each phrase below. If it is plural, write **PL** in the space. If it is singular possessive, write **SP**. If it is plural possessive, write **PP**.

1. PP the basketball players' jerseys
2. PL both of the referees
3. SP the home team's advantage
4. PP the fans' cheers
5. SP the stadium's location
6. PP the teams' coaches
7. PL the members of the team
8. PL the Minnesota Timberwolves

122

---

**Proof It**

Read the diary entry below. There are six plural possessives that are missing apostrophes or have apostrophes in the wrong places. Use proofreading marks to correct the errors.

| ℯ - deletes punctuation |
| ⌄ - inserts apostrophe |

October 18

Dear Diary,

Yesterday, I went to my first professional basketball game. The fans' screams were incredibly loud as the players jogged onto the court. The announcers' voices kept us informed of every play. At halftime, Dad and I went exploring. We brought our programs with us. I was hoping to run into some of the players and get autographs. No luck, though!

The last quarter of the game was very intense. Both teams' coaches looked worried. The Lakers were up by only two points, and I knew it was still anyone's game. There were large screens mounted all around the stadium. We could see the expressions on all the players' faces and every move they made.

With only three seconds remaining, the Lakers' forward made a free throw. I held my breath as the ball smoothly sailed through the net. The buzzers' sound signaled the end of the game. I can't wait to go to another pro game!

123

---

**Putting It Together**

Complete the chart below using the correct form of each noun.

| Singular | Plural | Plural Possessive | |
|---|---|---|---|
| zoo | zoos | zoos' | animals |
| loaf | loaves | loaves' | crusts |
| sheep | sheep | sheep's wool | |
| fairy | fairies | fairies' | wings |
| artist | artists | artists' paintings | |
| bush | bushes | bushes' branches | |
| clock | clocks | clocks' | hands |

Read the sentences below. There are nine mistakes with plurals. There are four mistakes with possessives. Use proofreading marks to correct the errors.

| ℯ - deletes letters and punctuation |
| ^ - inserts letters and punctuation |
| ⌄ - inserts apostrophes |

1. There are two pianos in the music room at Ross's school.
2. Three of the sopranos in the girls' choir have solos.
3. The choir director's sister gives trumpet lessons twice a week.
4. You can find the sheet music on the shelves in the closet.
5. There are so many varieties of instruments that Hitomi can't decide which to try next.
6. Each of the Blankenships' four children plays a different instrument.
7. After the performance, families can have some pastries and punch.

125

---

# Answer Key

---

A **subject pronoun** can be the subject of a sentence, or it can be part of a compound subject. *I, you, he, she, it, we,* and *they* are subject pronouns.

> *Eagles, hawks, owls, and vultures* are raptors.    *They* are raptors.
> *The Adventure Science Center* is in Nashville.    *It* is in Nashville.

When talking about yourself and someone else, always put the other person before you.

> *Grandpa and I* like to do crossword puzzles.
> *He and I* have a lot in common.

**Object pronouns** often follow action verbs or prepositions like *to, at, from, with,* and *of.* Some object pronouns are *me, you, him, her, it, us,* and *them.*

> Please give the DVDs to *Diego.*    Please give the DVDs *to him.*
> Gordon won *the race!*    Gordon *won it!*

If you use the pronoun *me* or *us* as part of a compound object, *me* or *us* comes after the other part of the compound.

> The day was exciting for our *parents and us.*

**Identify It**
Read the sentences below. The letters in parentheses will tell you to underline the subject pronoun (**SP**) or the object pronoun (**OP**).

1. My family and I went to the Foods of All Nations Festival. (SP)

2. We sampled foods from 13 countries. (SP)

3. Louis and Mom liked the Indian food best. They are going to make naan at home. (SP)

4. Dad loves Greek food. He has baked baklava for us many times. (OP)

5. Guacamole is a Mexican avocado dip. We ate it with fresh salsa and tortilla chips. (OP)

6. Jalapeño peppers are too spicy for Dad and me. (OP)

**126**

---

**Proof It**
Read the paragraphs below. Eight pronouns are used incorrectly. They may also be in the wrong places in the sentence. Use proofreading marks to correct the mistakes.

| ✐ – deletes words |
| ^ – inserts words |

Dad ordered some hummus at a Middle Eastern booth. It is made from ground chickpeas, and me and Louis weren't sure we'd like it. Dad gave us and Mom some hummus with pita bread. It was delicious.

Louis got some fried plantains and conch fritters at a Jamaican booth. Mom asked he what they tasted like. Him told her that the plantains tasted like bananas. He couldn't describe the conch fritters, so each tried one. Finally, it was time for dessert. Everyone in my family was feeling full, so us decided to order two dishes and share them. Trifle is an English dessert. It is made of sponge cake, custard, and fresh fruit. Dad also ordered some Japanese green-tea ice cream. Me and Mom loved it, but Louis thought it wasn't sweet enough. Tasting different foods at the festival made I think that I might like to be a chef someday.

**Try It**
On the lines below, write a short paragraph about some interesting foods you have tried or would like to try. Use one object pronoun and two subject pronouns in your paragraph. Underline the pronouns.

> Answers will vary.

**127**

---

Add **er** or **est** to an adjective to make a comparison.

> The giraffe is *taller* than the elephant.
> It is the *tallest* land mammal on Earth.

For adjectives that end in **e**, just add **r** or **st**. For adjectives that end in a consonant and a **y**, drop the **y** and add **ier** or **iest**.

> wise, wis**er**, wis**est**    fluffy, fluff**ier**, fluff**iest**    lonely, loneli**er**, loneli**est**

For some adjectives, double the final consonant before adding the ending.

> big, bi**gger**, bi**ggest**    thin, thi**nner**, thi**nnest**    dim, di**mmer**, di**mmest**

For adjectives that have two or more syllables, use more or most instead of adding an ending.

> She was the *most helpful* tour guide.
> Kim was *more excited* than Jamal.

Some comparative adjectives change completely with each form.

> good, better, best    bad, worse, worst

**Complete It**
Read each sentence below. Complete it with the correct comparative form of the adjective in parentheses.

1. On average, it is _____windier_____ on New Hampshire's Mount Washington than it is in Buffalo, New York. (windy)

2. The _____fastest_____ flying bird is the peregrine falcon. (fast)

3. Saffron is the _most expensive_ spice in the world. (expensive)

4. The world's _____largest_____ spider is the 11-inch long Goliath birdeater. (large)

5. It is usually _____wetter_____ in the Northwest than the Southwest. (wet)

**128**

---

**Proof It**
Read the paragraphs below. Find and correct the nine incorrect comparative adjectives.

| ✐ – deletes words |
| ^ – inserts words |

The students in Edward's class were trying to find a way to set a Guinness World Record. They decided that it wasn't a good idea to try to perform the dangerouser stunts. Anthony joked that he had the smelliest feet in the class. Simone said that she could eat spicier food than anyone she knew. Shankar and Katrina had a contest to see who could blow a bigger bubble with chewing gum. Their bubbles weren't even close in size to the biggest bubble ever blown.

"This is hard," said Edward, after hours of brainstorming. "We're not louder or faster or funnier or more amazing than any other kids," he said.

"I have an idea," said Katrina. "Could we be the most generous class? We could hold lots of fundraisers. We could volunteer for charity events. We could hold clothes drives and food drives."

"That's a great idea, Katrina," said Shankar. "I don't know if it's been done, but we can try to be the world's kindest class!"

**Try It**
Invent three new categories for world's records. Each category should include a comparative adjective. Write them on the lines below.

> Answers will vary.

**129**

---

Spectrum Language Arts
Grade 4
**192**

Answer Key

# Answer Key

---

**Page 130**

Like adjectives, adverbs can be used to make **comparisons**. Some adverbs follow the same rules that adjectives do. Add **er** or **est** to these adverbs to make a comparison.

The youngest boy worked *harder* than the other members of his team.

Darren jumped *highest*, but Kelley swam *faster*.

To make a comparison using adverbs that end in **ly**, add the words *more* or *most*.

Karim waited **more** *patiently* than his sister.

The stars seemed to shine **most** *brightly* when we were out in the country.

**Identify It**

Read each pair of sentences below. Circle the letter of the sentence in which the comparative adverb is used correctly.

1. (a.) Jamie recited his poem more calmly than the other contestants.
   b. Jamie recited his poem calmlier than the other contestants.

2. a. Nadia whispered most quietly than Kendall and Leo.
   (b.) Nadia whispered more quietly than Kendall and Leo.

3. a. The Randalls cheered more joyfully of all the families.
   (b.) The Randalls cheered most joyfully of all the families.

4. (a.) The fifth graders tried harder, but the fourth graders were faster.
   b. The fifth graders tried more hard, but the fourth graders were faster.

5. a. Maggie walked on the balance beam carefullier than the first two girls.
   (b.) Maggie walked on the balance beam more carefully than the first two girls.

---

**Page 131**

**Complete It**

Complete each sentence below with the correct comparative form of the adverb in parentheses.

1. Carly answers the phone **more cheerfully** than her brother. (cheerfully)

2. Out of all the fish in the sea, the sea horse swims the _____slowest_____. (slow)

3. Christopher listened to my long story **more patiently** than anyone else did. (patiently)

4. The Pandyas arrived _____sooner_____ than the Parkers or the Yamamotos. (soon)

5. Aunt Charlotte cooks __most skillfully__ of all her siblings. (skillfully)

6. The smallest puppy ate __more quickly__ than the other puppies from the same litter. (quickly)

7. My dad drives _____fastest_____ of any member of our family. (fast)

8. At the end of the long hike, Michelle raced to the lake __more eagerly__ than the other campers. (eagerly)

**Try It**

1. Write a sentence comparing two or more people or things. Use a form of the adverb *proudly*.

   _____

2. Write a sentence | Answers will vary. | or things. Use a form of the adverb *happily*.

   _____

---

**Page 132**

**Subject pronouns** are pronouns that can be used as the subject of a sentence. *I, you, he, she, it, we,* and *they* are subject pronouns.

*We* made fruit salad for the potluck dinner.   *He* is a tennis player.

**Object pronouns** often follow action verbs or prepositions. *Me, you, him, her, it, us,* and *them* are object pronouns.

Val called **them** yesterday.   The postcard is from **him**.

When talking about yourself (using the pronouns *I, me,* or *us*) and someone else, always put the other person before you.

*Taylor and I* are taking an art class.

To make a **comparison** using an adjective, do one of the following:
• add **er** or **est** (sweet, sweet**er**, sweet**est**)
• drop the **y** and add **ier** or **iest** (busy, bus**ier**, bus**iest**)
• double the final consonant before adding the ending (hot, hot**ter**, hot**test**)
• use *more* or *most* instead of adding an ending (**more** interesting)

To make a **comparison** using an adverb, do one of the following:
• add **er** or **est** to most short adverbs (yelled loud**er**, jumped high**est**)
• use *more* or *most* with adverbs ending in **ly** (**more** safely)

**Putting It Together**

Read the sentences below. Circle each pronoun. Write **SP** on the line if it is a subject pronoun. Write **OP** on the line if it is an object pronoun.

1. _SP_ Shalini and (I) posted signs for the dog wash.

2. _SP_ (We) placed the signs on bulletin boards all over town.

3. _OP_ Shalini's brothers helped (us) set everything up.

4. _OP_ Shalini thanked (them) for helping.

---

**Page 133**

Read the paragraphs below. They contain five mistakes with pronouns and seven mistakes with comparative adjectives and adverbs. Use proofreading marks to correct the mistakes.

It was sunnier on the day of the dog | – deletes words or letters / – inserts words or letters | wash than it had been all week.

Shalini and me had brought our hoses, shampoo, buckets, and towels to the park. We were ready to start washing, but no one came. Shalini waited more patient than I did, but both of we were anxious. Suddenly, three people arrived with their dogs, and me and Shalini were in business!

As the day went on, we became wetter and dirtier. The biggest dog we washed was a St. Bernard. Him was also the friendliest dog. He behaved most playfully than the other dogs when us sprayed him with water. By the end of the day, we were tired but proud. We had earned 60 dollars!

Fill in the spaces in the chart with the correct comparative form of the adjectives and adverbs.

| tiny | tinier | tiniest |
|---|---|---|
| bad | worse | worst |
| happily | more happily | most happily |
| clean | cleaner | cleanest |
| thin | thinner | thinnest |
| carefully | more carefully | most carefully |
| fluffy | fluffier | fluffiest |

---

Spectrum Language Arts
Grade 4

# Answer Key

---

**Synonyms** are words that have the same, or almost the same, meaning. Using synonyms can help you avoid repeating words and can make your writing more interesting.

| close, near | choose, select | break, shatter |
|---|---|---|
| yell, scream | sad, unhappy | grin, smile |

**Antonyms** are words that have opposite meanings.

| true, false | exciting, boring | rough, gentle |
|---|---|---|
| dark, light | shout, whisper | quickly, slowly |

**Identify It**

Read each sentence below. If the word in parentheses is a synonym for the underlined word, write **S** on the line. If it is an antonym, write **A**.

1. Anyone who <u>likes</u> caves should visit Mammoth Cave in Kentucky. (enjoys) **S**

2. Mammoth Cave is the <u>largest</u> cave system in the world. (smallest) **A**

3. The caves <u>stretch</u> for more than 350 miles. (extend) **S**

4. Echo River is on the <u>lowest</u> of the five levels. (highest) **A**

5. <u>Rare</u> types of crayfish and blind fish live in the river. (common) **A**

6. The caves are <u>always</u> about 54 degrees. (never) **A**

7. Mammoth Cave is one of the world's <u>amazing</u> natural wonders. (incredible) **S**

**Tip:** A **thesaurus** is a type of dictionary. Instead of containing definitions, it lists synonyms. A thesaurus can be a helpful tool for writers.

134

---

**Solve It**

Read the clues below. Choose the answers from the box, and write them in the numbered spaces in the crossword puzzle.

| difficult | below | different | narrow | strong |
|---|---|---|---|---|
| mistake | real | bravery | open | easy |

Across
1 antonym of *same*
4 synonym of *courage*
6 synonym of *error*
8 antonym of *closed*
9 synonym of *under*

Down
1 antonym of *easy*
2 antonym of *wide*
3 antonym of *weak*
5 antonym of *fake*
7 synonym of *simple*

**Try It**

1. Write a sentence using two of the following words: *giggle, grin, huge, wonderful, finish, break.*

2. Now, rewrite you ___ Answers will vary. ___ two words you chose.

135

---

**Homophones** are words that sound alike but have different spellings and meanings. Use the context of a sentence to decide which homophone to use.

We leave in *eight* hours.
*Their* dog keeps barking.
The opossum's *tail* is hairless.
Jackson *threw* the football.
Timmy *ate* the rest of the cereal.
*There* is the key!
I have heard you tell this *tale*.
The termites chewed *through* it.

**Complete It**

Read each sentence below. Circle the homophone from the pair in parentheses that correctly completes the sentence.

1. Praying mantises have sharp hooks on ((their) they're) legs.
2. If you walk around the garden with (bear, (bare)) feet, you might get stung by a bee.
3. The hummingbird sipped nectar from the brightly-colored (flour, (flower))
4. We planted two small ((pear,) pair) trees in the backyard.
5. If the ((weather,) whether) is nice tomorrow, we can plant the seedlings.
6. I already (new, (knew)) how to tell a ladybug from a cucumber beetle.

**Tip:** If you have trouble remembering which homophone is which, try making up a way to help yourself keep the meanings and spellings straight. For example, some people confuse the homophones *principal* and *principle*. To help yourself remember which is which, think of the school's princi**pal** as your *pal*.

136

---

**Proof It**

Read the flyer below. Thirteen homophones are used incorrectly. Use proofreading marks to correct the mistakes.

- ℓ - deletes words or letters
- ^ - inserts words or letters

WINDING CREEK GARDENING CENTER
1736 WELLSPRING ROAD
(842) 555-6824
LEARN HOW TO BUILD YOUR OWN BIRDHOUSE AT 2:00 ON SATURDAY, JUNE 20.
SUMMER SALE—SAVE 20% TO 50% find PLANTS AND GARDEN TOOLS.
YOU'LL find PLENTY OF BARGAINS.
WHY NOT PLANT SOME FLOWERING TREES AND BUSHES?
YOU'LL ENJOY THE scent ALL SUMMER LONG!
CHECK OUT our HERB AND VEGETABLE SEEDLINGS.
WE ALSO CARRY ALL KINDS OF GARDENING clothes,
INCLUDING HATS, SHOES, GLOVES, AND PANTS.
TAKE A MOMENT TO peek IN OUR GREENHOUSE
WHERE WE GROW RARE AND EXOTIC PLANTS.
THERE IS NO need TO HURRY—TAKE your time
AND ENJOY THE PLANTS.

**Try It**

On the lines below, write your own advertisement or flyer for a company you've invented. In your ad, use homophones for at least three of the following words: *ate, hour, won, reel, write, hole, hear, cell, wear, you're, sum, wood.*

Answers will vary.

137

---

Spectrum Language Arts
Grade 4
194

Answer Key

# Answer Key

**Multiple-meaning words**, also called **homographs**, are words that are spelled the same but have different meanings.

For example, *second* can mean *number two*, or it can mean *a moment in time*.

> The *second* book in the series is the best.
> I'll be finished in just a *second*.

The word *cold* can mean *an illness*, or it can mean *at a low temperature*.

> Parker caught a *cold* from Sydney.
> Use an ice pack to keep the food *cold*.

### Find It
The following dictionary entry shows two different meanings for the same word. Use it to answer the questions below.

> **bark** *noun* the outer layer of a tree
> *verb* the sound a dog makes

1. The *bark* of a birch tree is white and peels easily.
   Which definition of bark is used in this sentence? __a__
   **a.** the first definition          **b.** the second definition

2. The dog *barked* when he heard his owner's car in the driveway.
   Which definition of bark is used in this sentence? __b__
   **a.** the first definition          **b.** the second definition

3. What part of speech is *bark* when it is used to mean *the outer layer of a tree*? __a__
   **a.** a noun          **b.** a verb

4. Use the verb *bark* in a sentence.

Answers will vary.

138

---

### Rewrite It
Read each sentence below. Then, write a new sentence using a different meaning for the underlined word. Use a dictionary if you need help.

1. Tickets to the <u>fair</u> cost four dollars each.

2. I will meet you at the baseball <u>diamond</u> at 4:00.

3. The cast members of the <u>play</u> were excited about opening night.

4. <u>Coat</u> the inside      Answers will vary.

5. Mr. Armand works on the third <u>story</u> of the red brick building.

6. The small frog hid in the weeds that grew along the <u>bank</u> of the river.

### Try It
1. Write a sentence using a multiple-meaning word. Use *bat, train, patient, watch, leaves,* or another multiple-meaning word you know.

2. Now, write a sen      Answers will vary.      the word you chose.

139

---

**Synonyms** are words that have the same, or almost the same, meaning.
> answer, response          finish, complete          insect, bug

**Antonyms** are words that have opposite meanings.
> wide, narrow          never, always          capture, release

**Homophones** are words that sound alike but have different spellings and meanings.
> If it *rains*, we won't go.          Jen took the horse's *reins*.

**Multiple-meaning words**, also called **homographs**, are words that are spelled the same but have different meanings.
> The *leaves* are changing.          Enrique *leaves* in the morning.

### Putting It Together
Read each sentence below. Then, choose the sentence in which the underlined word is used the same way as it is in the first sentence. Write the letter of your answer on the line.

1. __a__ Did you receive the electric <u>bill</u> yet?
   **a.** The bill comes to $8.56.
   **b.** The duck has a longer bill than the sparrow.

2. __b__ My back hurts when I <u>lean</u> to the side.
   **a.** The runner was fit and lean.
   **b.** Lean the umbrella against the wall.

3. __b__ Laura's muscles are <u>firm</u> from the exercises she has been doing.
   **a.** There are six members of the law firm.
   **b.** The new mattress is nice and firm.

4. __a__ All the letters and papers are stored in a <u>trunk</u> in the attic.
   **a.** Belle found the costumes inside the trunk.
   **b.** The elephant uses its trunk in many ways.

140

---

Read each sentence below. If the word in bold print is used correctly, make a check mark on the line. If it is not used correctly, write its homophone on the line.

1. <u>see</u> It is hard to **sea** through all the fog.
2. __✓__ Sheila knew it was noon because the **sun** was directly overhead.
3. <u>pail</u> Duncan hung the **pale** on a peg in the barn.
4. __✓__ A row of **beech** trees led up to the house.
5. <u>whole</u> The **hole** family will attend the neighborhood party.
6. <u>blew</u> The wind **blue** hard and rattled the windows.
7. <u>break</u> If you **brake** the wood into small pieces, we can use it to start the fire.

Read each sentence below. If the underlined words are synonyms, write **S** on the line. If they are antonyms, write **A** on the line.

1. __A__ Dillon thought the puzzle would be <u>difficult</u>, but it was actually quite <u>easy</u>.
2. __S__ <u>Choose</u> the color you like best, and then let your brother <u>select</u> his favorite.
3. __A__ Would you rather we went <u>alone</u> or <u>together</u>?
4. __A__ Salim thought the painting looked <u>straight</u>, but as he stepped away, he could see that it was <u>crooked</u>.
5. __S__ The <u>amazing</u> athlete has performed many <u>incredible</u> feats.
6. __A__ If you place a <u>liquid</u> in the freezer, it will become a <u>solid</u> in just a few hours.

141

---

A **simile** is a figure of speech that compares two unlike things using the words *like* or *as*. Using similes in your stories or poems can make your writing stronger and more interesting to read. They allow the reader to form a vivid picture of what you are describing.

> Craig sanded the jagged edges until they were smooth.
> Craig sanded *the jagged edges* until they were *as smooth as marble*.

> The lawnmower growled as Celia pushed it across the lawn.
> *The lawnmower growled **like a hungry bear*** as Celia pushed it across the lawn.

**Identify It**

Read the paragraphs below. Find and underline the five similes.

Sumiko and Nori opened the door. The <u>fresh snow sparkled like chips of diamond</u> scattered across the front yard. Sumiko breathed in the fresh, icy air. When she exhaled, she could see the <u>cloud of breath hanging in the air like a small balloon.</u> Nori pulled on his scratchy wool mittens and joined Sumiko on the front step.

"This is amazing," said Nori, shaking his head as he looked around him. <u>Icicles hung like jewels from the trees.</u> There wasn't a single footprint or car track as far as he could see. The <u>outdoors was as quiet as a tomb</u>, except for the occasional crack as the sun melted an icicle and it dropped to the ground.

"Let's go for a walk," suggested Sumiko, as she put on her red knit hat. Sumiko and Nori set off down the quiet street, <u>the snow crunching like popcorn</u> beneath their feet.

142

---

**Complete It**

Complete each sentence below with a simile.

1. The field of wildflowers was as colorful _____
2. The balloon drifted gently through the air, like _____.
3. The tapping of rain on the tin roof was as comforting _____
4. Heath's stomach grumbled noisily, like _____
5. As Sara and Bret ~~Answers will vary.~~ hearts beat like
6. The rough, grainy sand felt like _____ on Ilana's bare feet.
7. The tart lemonade tasted as refreshing _____.
8. As he climbed the steps to the stage, Jacob was as nervous _____

**Try It**

Imagine yourself someplace far away. You may be on a beach just before a storm, in a crowded marketplace in a foreign country, or traveling down a river on a raft. On the lines below, write a short paragraph describing what you see. Use at least two similes in your paragraph.

_____

| Answers will vary. |

_____

143

---

Like a simile, a **metaphor** is a figure of speech that can be used to make a piece of writing more interesting. Use a metaphor to make a comparison without using the words *like* or *as*.

> *Alejandro's short hair* was *a small, sleek cap* perched on his head.
> *Mrs. Gallo* is *a mother hen* to all the children in the neighborhood.
> *The students* were *busy bees* as they prepared for the guest's arrival.

**Identify It**

Read each sentence below. If it contains a simile, circle it and write **S** on the line. If it contains a metaphor, circle it and write **M** on the line.

1. **M** The fireflies were tiny stars in the dark blue sky.
2. **S** Worry filled the room like a cloud of smoke.
3. **M** The crickets were talented musicians that filled the night with music.
4. **S** The summer air smelled as sweet as cotton candy.
5. **M** Terrance's fingers were rubber as he desperately worked to untie the knots.
6. **M** The exhausted boy was a robot as he slowly made his way up the stairs to bed.
7. **S** The waves were like wild animals as they leaped at the expert surfer.
8. **M** Excitement was an electric current that ran through the stadium.
9. **S** Chelsea's eyes are as blue as the inside of the McIntyres' pool.

144

---

**Complete It**

Read each metaphor below. Then, fill in the lines to show which two things are being compared.

Example: To Eli, the shrieking sirens were fingernails on a chalkboard.
    __shrieking sirens__ compared to __fingernails on a chalkboard__

1. The falling leaves were confetti swirling in the air.
    __falling leaves__ compared to __confetti__
2. The soap bubbles were pearls scattered along the edge of the tub.
    __soap bubbles__ compared to __pearls__
3. The tornado was a dinosaur that roared terribly at anything in its path.
    __tornado__ compared to __dinosaur__
4. Although the air was cold, the sunlight was a blanket that warmed the cold children.
    __sunlight__ compared to __blanket__
5. The train was a bullet that shot through the tunnel at more than 70 miles an hour.
    __train__ compared to __bullet__

**Try It**

On the lines below, write two metaphors. You can begin your sentences with ideas from the box, or you can use ideas of your own.

| The thunderstorm was | The morning sun is | The tiny kitten was |

1. _____
2. _____ Answers will vary.

145

---